THE NEXT

The Decline and Rise of the United States

AMERICA

Michael Harrington/Photographs by Bob Adelman

Designed by Neil Shakery

HOLT, RINEHART AND WINSTON   NEW YORK

Published by Holt, Rinehart and Winston,
383 Madison Avenue, New York, New York 10017.

Published simultaneously in Canada by Holt, Rinehart and
Winston of Canada, Limited.

Library of Congress Cataloging in Publication Data

Harrington, Michael.
  The next America.

  1. United States—Social conditions—1945–
2. United States—Politics and government—1945–
3. Radicalism—United States. I. Adelman, Robert.
II. Title
HN58.H245   1981   973.92   81-1086
ISBN Hardbound: 0-03-057468-4   AACR2
ISBN Paperback: 0-03-057467-6 (An Owl book)

First Edition
Produced by Bob Adelman
Printed in the United States of America by Rapaport Printing Co. in the Stonetone process.
Bound by Sendor Bindery, New York

THE NEXT
AMERICA

BY MICHAEL HARRINGTON
The Other America
The Retail Clerks
The Accidental Century
Toward a Democratic Left
Socialism
Fragments of the Century
Twilight of Capitalism
The Vast Majority
Decade of Decision

BY BOB ADELMAN
Down Home
Gentlemen of Leisure
(with Susan Hall)

The next America is at hand, inevitable and indeterminate. The last America, a coherence inherited from the 1930s, is going, going, almost gone. The problem is, there are several next Americas which have now become possible, some of them frightening, one of them worth at least two cheers and a passionate commitment. The Presidential election of 1980 was a confused, appalling recognition of this fact. The voters turned away from an exhausted liberalism which could not cope with an unprecedented crisis of simultaneous and chronic inflation-recession. There were, to be sure, historic accidents at work in the event. Ironically, the used-up liberalism was represented by Jimmy Carter, who had never identified with it when it was truly relevant. And since Carter had spent four years making the worst of a bad situation, the Republicans attacked him from the left as well as the right: "If the Democratic party is the party of the working people, why are so many people not working?" It was the year of the young fogy. But the 1980 elections were not simply a referendum on economic policy. To the extent that they were, Ronald Reagan was elected because he was not Jimmy Carter and seemed to be a nice person. But Reagan was also a conservative utopian, the visionary candidate in the race. He spoke of America as "the city on the hill," a phrase taken from the Puritan theocrat, John Winthrop, who had dreamed of a Massachusetts Bay Colony as a harmonious society permeated by the spiritual. Reagan's nostalgia for that three-hundred-year-old simplicity touched a late-twentieth-century electorate teetering on the edge of an uncertain future. It resonated because the nation intuitively knew that its plight was not simply a matter of devalued dollars but also, to borrow from Nietzsche, of devalued values.

So Reagan talked of the old verities, of work, family, neighborhood and peace. He understood that the current crisis was cultural and existential as well as economic. As a committed socialist I could not agree more with this conservative premise. Indeed, it informs this book. That is why I have worked with Bob Adelman, trying to evoke our situation through his pictures as well as denote it in my text, suggesting an atmosphere which enshrouds the facts. And it is why I circle around our predicament, using bits of autobiography along with statistics and trends. But how can I, in this year zero of a seemingly renascent conservatism, then go on to argue that the next America must be found well to the left of the New Deal rather than in a return to Herbert Hoover? What serious justification is there for such a quixotic quest? Because John Winthrop's hill was bulldozed long ago to make way for a suburban shopping center; because conservative utopias are not simply irrelevant but the charming façade of modern reaction. I will show—not frivolously or disrespectfully—that the "city on the hill" has turned into a corporate fairy tale in central Florida called Disney World, where Cinderella's Castle fronts for an efficient monopoly. In other words, the conservative fantasies may come true, but only if the conservative values are gutted in the process. And the dream of honorable work and stable families, of neighborhood communities and a world at peace, can be realized only if the nation goes beyond the old liberalism, taking the best of its accomplishments along with it. That is why I think the various disintegrations of these times—including the passing of the last generation's liberalism—may signal not decline and fall, but decline and rise.

M.H.

DECLINE

February 24, 1977. It was my forty-ninth birthday, which put me in a thoughtful mood. It was also bone-chilling and wet as I walked across Greenwich Village in the early-evening darkness. Panhandlers accosted me; junkies huddled in doorways near their haunt on Sixth Avenue and Eighth Street; a graying, burly black man stood with a liquor bottle in his hand, mumbling incoherently, oblivious of the rain. **I** remember earlier evenings. The disorder I encountered in the Greenwich Village of 1949 had been orderly. The drinking, the flouting of established sexual mores and the breaking of literary and artistic rules were all part of a serious, often joyous, commitment to antivalues. Our "immorality" was thus a morality in disguise. But the human degradation I observed on this birthday is not calculated or whimsical or aesthetic. It is a fate, not a choice, one more by-product of the urban (the societal?) disintegration in which I—and millions of New Yorkers—live. **A**re my friends and I, the radical critics of this system, partly responsible for these shattered people? I know, of course, about the massive economic trends that are destroying New York, about the exodus of hundreds of thousands of jobs, more often than not facilitated by federal subsidies, and the inflow of displaced persons, more often than not the victims of federal agricultural policies, from the fields of the South and from Puerto Rico. I have documented how wrong Richard Nixon was when he said that the sixties failed because we "threw money at problems." **A**nd yet.

We radicals had mocked the old verities and preached a new freedom, only our negatives were more powerful than our creativity. One reason was that our anti-establishment iconoclasm had been aristocratic. We proposed that men and women find their purpose within themselves, that they disdain all the traditional crutches, like God and flag. But were we then to blame because many seemed to have heard only that the old constraints had been abolished and ignored the call to find new obligations on their own? **S**everal years after that walk in the rain, I ran across a comment by George Orwell which marvelously summarized the insight I had been groping for. Orwell was talking about the intellectual attack on religion: "For two hundred years we had sawed and sawed at the branch we were sitting on. And in the end, much more suddenly than anyone had foreseen, our efforts were rewarded and down we came. But unfortunately there had been a little mistake. The thing at the bottom was not a bed of roses after all, it was a cesspool full of barbed wire." Orwell had in mind the totalitarian societies which had emerged out of the ruins of secular messianism, but his point applies to all of the disillusionments of this enlightened, secular age. **I** think of a particular case in point which has troubled me from time to time. Martin Luther King, Jr., was among the greatest Americans of the century, and it had been one of my highest privileges to have worked with him personally, even if not intimately. I had participated in some of his nonviolent campaigns in which masses of people were called upon to violate unjust laws in the name of true legality. But had King, and the rest of us, thereby persuaded at least some among the

Derelict, Bowery, New York City, 1978

Confessed juvenile killer, Harlem, New York City, 1978

minorities that therefore no laws were binding, that everything was permissible? Was our higher justice an incentive to common crime? **T**wo days after my rainy walk, I raised that question with Betty Rollin, a friend who is an NBC television reporter. She had done a series on teen-age criminals, some of whom had committed murder (but had not been arrested for that crime). We talked about those young people. One of them, she said, did not know his own birthday; none of them could read; all of them came from homes in which love was, at the very best, sporadic, interspersed with rejection and violence. At the age of fourteen or fifteen, we agreed, their lives were already programmed for personal and social disaster. It would take a miracle to keep them from a life of rape, criminality and prison. **W**ere they motivated by race hatred? I asked. Had King's subversion of illegitimate authority led them to turn on all forms of authority? Not that she could tell, Betty replied. They didn't seem to even be aware of the civil rights movement or of King; they would kill a black without remorse as well as a white, for it was life, all life, that they held to be cheap. So things are more complex than I had imagined; perhaps I had been too quick to confess my own guilt. **T**he walk through the Village and the conversation with Betty Rollin occurred when I was beginning to think about the themes of this book. I had seen decline personified in the ruined figures who had replaced the ebullient outcasts on the streets of the Village, but I had also learned that there were no quick, easy theories to explain that transition. The resultant sense of complexity led to some speculations, which underlie everything that follows.

Cultures are never things; they are always alive with contrary possibilities. For two centuries, during which humani-

Family of welfare recipients, Brooklyn, New York, 1978

ty's technological marvels have transformed the very surface of the globe, there's always been reason for pessimism. Because, as Immanuel Kant was perhaps the first to realize, the prodigies of science and industry dramatize the impotence of the spirit; the micro- and macroscopic certitudes about our external world contrast cruelly with the anguished doubts about our inner selves. Because, as Karl Marx knew, our triumphs were purchased at a price of unplanned and unpredictable change and our ingenuity therefore made us insecure. **S**o even in the midst of unprecedented accomplishments, an individual could take a despairing view of reality. Or, to complicate matters even more, geniuses could prescribe contrary cures for a cultural malady they defined in the same way. A Nietzsche and a Marx could both understand the essential hypocrisy of the bourgeois society in which they lived. They differed only with regard to the essential. The one despised the people, whom he saw as the source of even further debasements of civilization; the other saw in them the principle of a new civilization. Similarly, entire epochs can differ within themselves. The 1950s, with their celebration of the glories of America, were as authentic a manifestation of the national spirit as the sixties, with their liberal and radical critiques of the system. As were the seventies, with their foreboding of decline, which seeped through the public consciousness like the smell of gas. **T**he seventies. These were years of in-between. Some of the most basic of the old truths—about religion and art and sex as well as politics and economics—decayed, but there are no new truths to take their place. Long ago, Alfred de Musset described the "sickness of the century" in which he lived: "All that was is no longer; all that will be is not yet." So it is now. Another way of put-

Looting, South Bronx, New York, 1978

View from Charlotte Street, South Bronx, New York, 1981

Family, South Bronx, New York, 1976

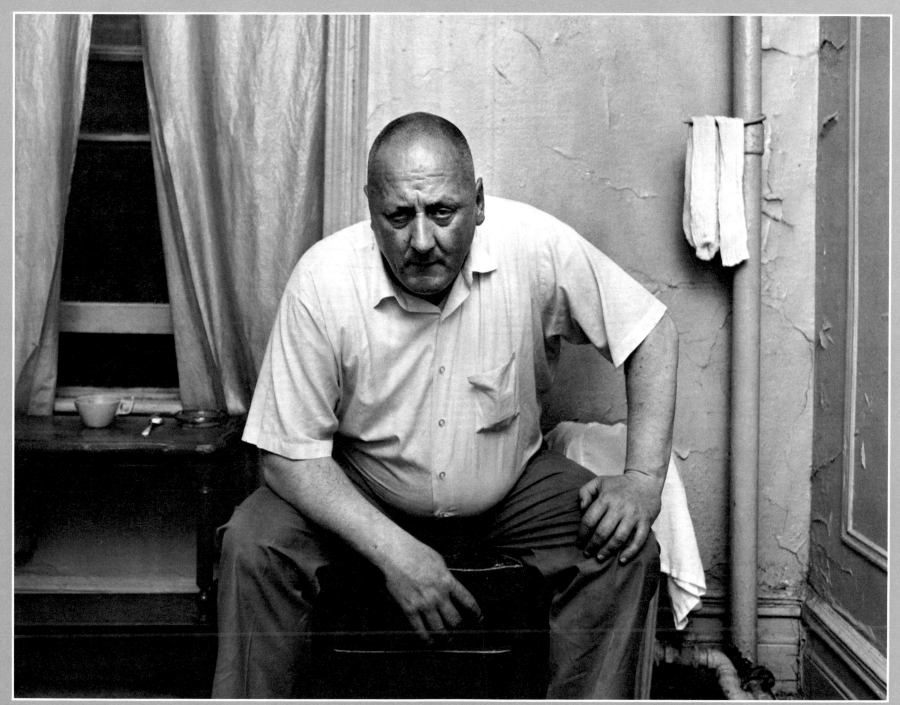

Transient-hotel occupant, New York City, 1978

Lower East Side, New York City, 1975

Glue sniffer, South Bronx, New York, 1978

Lower East Side, New York City, 1975

ting the same thought: many of the most important long-run contradictions of our society have suddenly emerged as short-run problems. The long run, John Maynard Keynes once said contemptuously, is a subject for undergraduates—that is, something vague and imprecise, fit for beery generalizations late at night, immune to empirical challenge. Only now, if I am right, the long run is a daily experience of most of the people in America. **I** tried to document and analyze the economics and politics of that development in *Decade of Decision*. Here, the data are cultural, personal, even intimate, but they are as important a trend as shifts in the GNP. Within the past ten or so years, sexuality, politics, and religion have simultaneously come unstuck, along with the economy, and no new synthesis has come to take their place.

The economy produces too much; the economy doesn't produce nearly enough. **T**he first part of this contradiction was a cultural cliché of the sixties, yet it has real content. From the beginning of human society until the late nineteenth century—a period twelve millennia long—the overwhelming majority of humankind barely managed to exist. Life was, indeed, brutish and short. Then, around 1880, some of the direct producers in the Western capitalist countries raised themselves above a subsistence income. The event did not come automatically, as the gift of the new technology. It was the result of a gigantic increase in productivity *and* the most bitter class struggles. **A**fter World War II, there was another dramatic break in the historic trend line. As the Keynesian revolution triumphed, governments encouraged—within unspoken, but very real, limits—mass consumption in order to guarantee outlets for the production controlled by the rich. Hedonism became an essential dictate of public policy.

The idea was not new. As far back as the early eighteenth century, Bernard Mandeville had argued in *The Fable of the Bees* that "bare virtue can't make nations live in splendor." Pleasure seeking, he said, was economically functional, even necessary. To put it mildly, Mandeville was ahead of his time; in 1723, his book was convicted as a nuisance by a Middlesex grand jury. The notion of the value of "unproductive consumption" did surface in Malthus's writing in the early nineteenth century as a rationale for middle-class luxury, but the mainstream economists ignored this aberration and Marx abominated it. It was not until Keynes prevailed in the thirties that this heresy became the orthodoxy of both statesmen and academics.

Queens, New York, 1968

In the 1960s, the American government adopted the consumption ethic with a vengeance. The new economics of the Kennedy-Johnson years did not stimulate economic growth by direct public investments in socially useful goods and services. Rather, it gave income to private buyers in a corporate market by means of tax cuts. So an individual making a purchase was fulfilling a civic duty. There was, the sociologist Daniel Bell later wrote, a "cultural contradiction" in the reformed capitalism: on the one hand, the system encouraged self-expression and -indulgence so that it could sell the products of its ingenuity; on the other hand, it demanded scientific rigor and austerity in order to maintain that ingenuity.

It was no accident that the counterculture developed at this point. The new affluence subverted that most ancient principle of societal discipline: who does not work shall not eat. Millions of Americans, and billions of people around the globe, were excluded from this liberation.

Mall, Paramus, New Jersey, 1981

Central Park, New York City, 1978

New York City, 1978

Massage demonstration, Coliseum, New York City, 1977

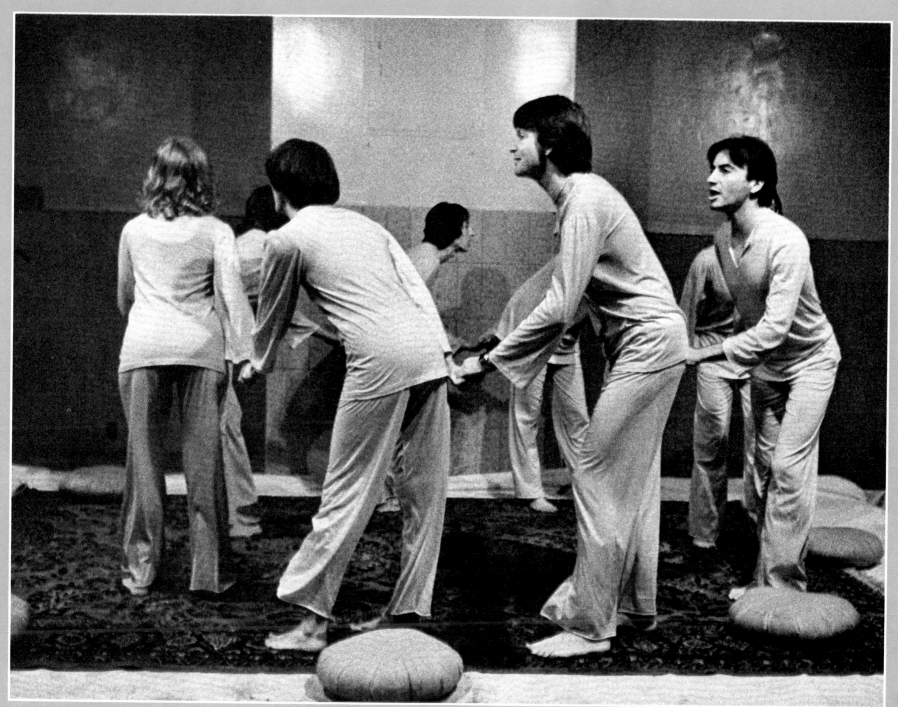

Arica exercise, Coliseum, New York City, 1977

Pyramid power, Coliseum, New York City, 1977

Eric Sloane, painter, Kent, Connecticut, 1976

But many in the largest generation in this country's history experienced it. So protest against bourgeois morality, which was permeated by the old assumptions about scarcity, became a kind of conformity. To take one example: marijuana, which had once been the province of tiny groups in the demimonde, became, in less than a decade, as ubiquitous as beer. **T**his generation in American life lasted about eight years. As he left office in January 1969, Lyndon Johnson proudly told the nation that the economy was no longer a "relentless tide of ups and downs." This was the unspoken creed of the sixties, the premise of all of its life-styles. An endless, noninflationary, conflict-free growth would allow Presidents to prosecute undeclared wars and young people to drop out with comfort. This was a time when there were even, to use Irving Howe's trenchant phrase, "guerrillas with tenure." **T**hen Richard Nixon came into office in 1969 and the economy seemed to be nothing but a relentless tide of ups and downs. There was a roller-coaster ride of boom and bust, and in clear contravention of the new economic truths, the worst inflation of the century and the worst recession in a generation occurred at the same time. Suddenly, politicians discovered that Small Is Beautiful and gave sermons on how the government could not satisfy the expectations it had excited. The old-fashioned economic contradictions of capitalism asserted themselves. **B**ut the return of the familiar crises did not revive the old psychology. A generation had spent its most impressionable years learning that it was exempt from the immemorial restraints. When it turned out that the material preconditions of that attitude no longer existed, the attitude did not die. It became frustrated and angry. Moreover, the counterculture had conquered a good

New York, 1968

New York City, 1968

part of the nations's spiritual space with incredible speed. Within less than a decade, mores that were the bizarre behavior of a vanguard in New York's East Village or San Francisco's Haight-Ashbury appeared everywhere between the two coasts. **H**ere, then, is one characteristic, contradictory pattern of the seventies. In the late sixties, the fashionable philosophers wondered if America could cope with the dangers of abundance; in 1980, they discussed the limits of scarcity. Epochs lasted less than ten years, it was unclear whether we had too much or not enough, and in fact we had both at the same time.

The contraries were not confined to the public sphere. They penetrated to the intimate core of private lives. In sexuality, for instance, people in the seventies became more libertine and remained stubbornly traditionalist. **I**t is obvious that the new developments in sexual morality during the seventies had been building for some time. In the middle distance, for instance, Kinsey's epochal study in the 1940s had described a change in attitude among younger people. There was more nudity, more variety in sexual practice, more foreplay and more orgasm. In contrast to the generation of the twenties, a fifth or more of the younger women in the forties were having orgasms most, or all, of the time during intercourse. The official frigidity of Victorianism was clearly giving way to a more permissive, hedonistic spirit. But then there was a new, and sharp, turning in the 1960s. Changed attitudes suddenly became changed practices. **T**his process suggests a hypothesis. One of the most fascinating aspects of the contemporary world is the speed with which ideas diffuse from a cultural vanguard to the mass of people. The emotions felt by the

Costume party, New York City, 1970

New York City, 1978

Lost Generation in Paris in the twenties were known to hordes of college students by the sixties; the Cubism which shocked the middle class before World War I inspired wallpaper patterns after World War II; and the sexual mores of the Freudian Left and Bohemia between the two wars became commonplace for almost all youth by the seventies. In the case of the sexual shift, the development seems to have divided into two phases. First people began to talk and think in a new way, and the old order was demolished in theory. Then—and this is what happened in the mid-sixties—they actually began to act in a new way. This shift has little to do with the lurid accounts of "swinging"—of mate swapping, orgies and all the rest— that so obsessed the pseudo-liberated, prurient press. Morton Hunt, the author of an important survey study, "Sexual Behavior in the 1970s," notes that this kind of conduct is limited to a minority. The data might even show that it is in decline in the seventies.* Hunt adds an interesting footnote: most of the swingers were political and social conservatives, Middle Americans rather than decadent elitists. One sophisticated respondent who engaged in "swinging" told Hunt that he was appalled at the uncultured people he encountered in his adventures. However, my main concern here is not with swingers but with the majority of Americans, a remarkable number of whom changed their sexual practices during the last ten years. This is how Hunt describes the transition: "during the past generation a major—and permanent—reevaluation of sexual attitudes has been occurring throughout our society, a process that has left its

Nude beach, Gateway National Park, New York, 1979

*Hunt's survey was done for *Playboy* magazine, hardly a scholarly or disinterested source. Another study which will be cited here was done for *Redbook* magazine. But despite the popular audience for which both were intended, the data were gathered in a scientific fashion and can be taken seriously.

After-hours club, New York City, 1978

After-hours club, New York City, 1978

mark on each age group and recorded its history in the form of growing attitudinal permissiveness and behavioral liberalism of the younger groups." "To the majority of Americans," he writes, "sexual liberation . . . means the right to enjoy all parts of the body, the right to employ caresses previously forbidden by civil or religious edict and social tradition, and the right to be sensuous and exuberant rather than perfunctory and solemn—but all within the framework of meaningful relationships." **F**or example, in 1953 Kinsey found that only 33 percent of women over twenty-five had had premarital intercourse. In a 1975 survey of 100,000 women by *Redbook* magazine, the figure had risen to 90 percent. In that age group, Kinsey found that 9 percent had had extramarital intercourse; in the *Redbook* study, the figure was 25 percent. Obviously, one of the remarkable things about these statistics is the speed with which they were transformed. "In the quarter of a century since the present sexual era began with the publication of the first 'Kinsey Report,'" Hunt remarks, "the changes in sexual attitude and in sexual behavior in America have been of such proportions as have historically required one to several centuries to take place." **I**ndeed, we may

After-hours club, New York City, 1978

even be able to pinpoint the shift as having taken place in the mid-sixties. A study of Catholic attitudes in America directed by Andrew Greeley, a priest and sociologist, points very much in the direction of that date. In 1963, Greeley and his colleagues write, "only 29 percent [of the national sample of Catholics] agreed strongly with the notion that husband and wife may have sexual intercourse for pleasure alone. That proportion has now [in 1973] risen to 50 percent. Remarriage after divorce was approved by 52 percent a decade ago; it is now approved by 73 percent . . . . Sexual relations between an engaged couple was approved by only 12 percent in 1963; it is

After-hours club, New York City, 1978

After-hours club, New York City, 1977

now approved by 43 percent." **S**o three surveys show that a sharp change occurred in sexual attitudes and practice, and one of them suggests that it happened sometime in the mid-sixties. The Catholic figures are particularly compelling since they describe a profound modification in attitude among a population that, only yesterday, had made observance of a strict sexual code a crucial determinant of religious ortho-doxy. This is not, of course, to say that the events of the past ten years are sufficient to explain what happened. During the past several centuries—from the eighteenth-century libertines in France, through the Romantics, the Bohemians, the Freudians and many other intellectual and cultural tendencies—there has been an attack on traditional Western sexual moral-ity. What is relevant to this analysis of these times of in-between is that this long-range trend erupted into the lives of millions of Americans during the past ten years. **A**nd yet this revolution was not as unambiguous as I have thus far made it seem. Hunt's data indicate that the very people who are now acting in new ways are still searching for sex within a context of emotion and affection. The marriage and divorce statistics bear on his analysis. Between 1910 and 1970, the rate of marriages per one thousand Americans remained stable (it did drop, for obvious reasons, during the Great Depression, but rebounded immediately after the economic crisis ended), while the divorce rate rose fivefold. People remained com-mitted to the ancient institution of the family and to the romantic ideal of love even as they redefined both.

The resultant tension may well have been prefigured in a book that Bertrand Russell wrote in 1929, *Marriage and Morals*. Russell quite accurately predicted that the decline of religious belief and the development of effective contraceptives were subverting the two chief props of middle-class morality, the fear of hellfire and pregnancy. Moreover, he advocated an open and healthy sexuality as well as trial marriage, positions that were so radical in the "roaring" twenties that the city of New York refused to let such a freethinker teach at one of its colleges. Yet in the same book, Russell worried that the new sexuality might degrade itself into triviality and insisted upon the need to put sex into an emotional, and even a spiritual, context. **S**o the new freedom arrived abruptly and was filled with inner tensions. It was related to another change, one that the conservative sociologist Robert Nisbet has called the "most fundamental of modern revolutions": the drive for women's liberation. It can be said, Nisbet argued, that "an entire civilization, in the West certainly, reflects in countless ways the historic acceptance of women's inferiority to the male." That primordial proposition was challenged in the seventies. And ironically, this subversion of the most venerable discrimination in human life was brought about casually, as a by-product of society's new dedication to mass consumption. **T**here has been a certain pattern in feminist activism in American history: it is usually set in motion by women's involvement in the struggle for someone else's emancipation. The first upheaval took place in the 1850s, and it was stimulated by women's participation in the abolitionist fight against slavery. The second surge occurred in the period leading up to World War I, and it was part of the socialist and progressive ferment. The third incarnation of the movement dates from the late sixties, and its militants were, in large measure, drawn from, or inspired by, the civil rights and antiwar campaigns. In each of these three cases, women came to understand their own oppression

West Feliciana, Louisiana, 1964

Debutante party, Dallas, Texas, 1966

by first becoming conscious of the oppression of another group. **A**nd yet the revival of feminism in the seventies is not to be explained solely, or perhaps even primarily, in terms of the consciousness of its activists, important as that was and is. It was also the consequence of economic and social trends in which men unwittingly promoted a sexual egalitarianism which many of them later found appalling.

It all began during World War II, when the society desperately needed women in war production because fifteen million men were in uniform. When the peace came, some of these women returned to the role of "homemaker" and to the "feminine mystique"—that idealization of the inferior place of women in terms of the "higher" values of motherhood, nurturing, femininity and the like. Many analysts expected the returning male veterans to have something of a fling when they got home. Instead, they married, embracing domesticity with a passion. The "baby boom" was one result. **B**ut the countertrend continued. More and more women took jobs. The "affluent society" of the fifties—which is to say, the semi-affluent society, with an underworld of the poor and a majority having trouble making ends meet—was supposed to make everyone contented, passive, nonideological. In fact, it literally forced wives into the labor market, since many families could not participate in the consumer competition unless they had two incomes. And that necessity, which arose out of a system that was supposed to tranquilize everyone, became a major source of discontent. **T**he reason was simple enough, even though it took a while to impress itself upon the consciousness of those who suffered from it. Women did not simply enter the labor market. They did so under conditions

New York City, 1970

New York City, 1970

similar to those imposed on blacks and other minorities. They were concentrated in low-paying service and clerical jobs; they were the last hired and therefore the first fired; their "background characteristics," above all the fact that they typically interrupted their careers to have, and care for, children, disqualified them from the best opportunities and subjected them to active discrimination. The first awareness of this systematic injustice arose, again quite ironically, within Left-wing movements. There the women activists discovered that they were supposed to occupy the same subordinate position—as cooks, typists, sex objects—that they were assigned in middle-class society. Their realization of radical hypocrisy on this count was a factor that provoked them to a global critique of the female's second-class status in all of American life. The first stirrings occurred primarily among the college-educated and committed women who had gravitated to protest movements. As a result, there were some who dismissed them as unimportant dilettantes, as exponents of radical chic. Overlooked was the fact that this vanguard was articulating grievances that were deeply embedded in the lives of a majority of American women. Some of the most striking gains were made on behalf of that majority: a successful suit against the phone company helped telephone operators, most of whom were anything but elite Leftists.

So the new consciousness of sex roles was not confined to the educated middle (or upper-middle) class. Some of Hunt's statistics are particularly interesting in this regard. Kinsey had discovered a marked social class difference in sexual practices. The incidence of oral-genital sex, for instance, correlated with education and was much more common among the college-educated (which would be one rough indicator of

New York City, 1968

Dallas, Texas, 1966

New York City, 1968

middle-class status) than among working people. One of the things that happened between Kinsey's studies in the forties and early fifties and Hunt's survey in the seventies is that the social class factors all but disappeared from the sex lives of the American people. Class differentials, as in Kinsey's oral-sex findings, no longer existed. And just as a change in sexual attitudes and practices thus moved from the cultural elite to the vast majority, so the consciousness of women's exploited position in the society and the demand for a redefinition of roles moved rapidly from vanguard to mass. **T**he seventies, then, experienced two profound, contradictory revolutions, in sexuality and in sex roles. Each was sudden; each was ambiguous. Meanwhile, American politics were moving vigorously left, right and center. The people were disillusioned with politics in general, which was the source of a conservative mood; they were forced, by some of the same factors that had led them to a generalized disenchantment, to politicized, and even radical, attitudes about the particulars. Here again, dissonance was the dominant sound.

In the established academic theory of American politics in the post–World War II period, one could make a great deal of sense out of the nation's past. But as the seventies proceeded, that theory could not cope with the present and the immediate future, or rather, insofar as it did it saw only puzzling departures and uncertain outcomes. The average person in the street is not a political scientist, yet he or she participated viscerally in a breakdown of political loyalties which coincided, as will be seen, with a decline in religious faith. And that same person was simultaneously forced to become more political. **A**ccording to the established theory, American politics are remarkably stable. Every forty or fifty

Democratic National Convention, Atlantic City, New Jersey, 1964

years, there is a "realigning," or "critical," election in which a new majority coalition asserts itself. In the 1890s, the Republicans, the party of triumphant capitalism, assumed control; in the 1930s, the Democrats, the party of the welfare state, took over. In between, national elections simply reinforced this coalition structure. There can be, to be sure, "deviating" elections in which some particular circumstance—the Republican split in 1912, which led to a three-way race and the Presidency of Woodrow Wilson—gives rise to an exception. Still, the main fact of political life is its stability, and ordinarily the characteristic that best predicts how a person will vote is how his or her father voted. This analysis worked brilliantly from the origins of the party system to 1964. But after that, the data simply did not fit the theory. It was in 1964 that Lyndon Johnson won by such a landslide that there was widespread speculation on whether the event marked the end of the Republican party. By March 1968, Johnson's fortunes were in such a shambles that he, in effect, resigned from the reelection that he normally could have taken for granted. Then in 1972, Nixon won his landslide—but two counterpoised landslides within eight years is not exactly political stability. Less than two years later, Nixon himself was forced out of office because of Watergate. In the process, the American people got a tape-recorded glimpse of the immoralities and vulgarities of power during his administration.

White House, Washington, D.C., 1981

America had believed in Lyndon Johnson and he led the nation into the bloody swamp of Vietnam, where it never should have been in the first place. The people never believed in Richard Nixon—he was probably the most unpopular man ever to win an overwhelming victory—yet they accepted him as a lesser evil. And he dragged them through the mud of the Watergate scandal even as he presided over the worst unem-

Democratic National Convention, New York City, 1976

White House, Washington, D.C., 1981

New York City, 1976

ployment and inflation in a generation. Small wonder that cynicism and disenchantment with politics became rampant in the seventies and that various polls reported a sharp decline in the perceived legitimacy of all the official institutions of the society. **I**f these bewildering events were the only problems for the prevailing theory of political behavior, they could be explained away, even though that would require considerable ingenuity. It might be said that both 1964 and 1972 were simply deviating elections: 1964 because the Republicans moved so far to the right with Goldwater, 1972 because the Democrats lurched so far to the left with McGovern. In such a consoling analysis, the American people would remain firmly in the center, which is where, this country has believed for a long time, a gracious providence has located the proper answer to all questions. The vast mass, it could then be said, are still stable; only the parties are erratic.

Unfortunately for orthodoxy, there were more data. They were even more anomalous, from the point of view of the conventional wisdom, than the two contradictory landslides within eight years. The surveys recorded a marked decline in party loyalty. The Republicans fell to a hard core of about 20 percent of the electorate; the Democrats dropped below 50 percent; the independents became the second largest contingent on the electoral rolls. So it was that in the campaign of 1976, politicians who ran on an antipolitics platform—Jimmy Carter and Jerry Brown—scored surprising successes in the Democratic Presidential primaries. **T**he result, the political scientist Walter Dean Burnham suggests, could be a "politics without parties." In such a perspective, there would be frequent and unpredictable gyrations of the electorate. Personality would come to count more than program. All this would

New York City, 1968

New York City, 1968

Washington, D.C., 1968

Atlantic City, New Jersey, 1964

occur at a time when the basic position of America in the world economy would be more in question than at any time since the Great Depression, when the cities of the Northeast and the Midwest were falling apart, and when there would be more than a little public sense of aimlessness and confusion with regard to basic goals. A society challenged in its essentials, desperately needing to confront and resolve deep structural problems, would have lost the political capacity for the intelligent, organized discussion of anything. **H**ere is Arthur Schlesinger's pessimistic assessment of what this could mean: "We might then enter an era in which political leaders, like Chinese warlords, roam the countryside, organizing personal armies . . . conducting hostilities against some rival warlords and forming alliances with others and, as they win elections, striving to govern through ad hoc coalitions in legislatures. . . . Without parties our politics could grow angrier, wilder and more irresponsible." **W**hy does this disquieting possibility exist? Why have American party loyalties eroded so dramatically in recent years, thus contributing to the sickness of the decade? **R**ichard Nixon had an answer. On the day after his re-election in 1972, he developed it in an extremely influential interview in the *Washington Star*. During the sixties, he said, the upper class had gone soft, become permissive and started "throwing money at problems." This, in turn, had bred irresponsibility among the masses, particularly among the young. It was, he argued, one of the major reasons for the growth in drug addiction. The people, he concluded, needed to be treated sternly, as if they were children, and the government must withdraw from areas of the society into which it had wrongly intervened. Only in that way would Americans once more become self-reliant.

New York City, 1974

Transient-hotel occupant, New York City, 1978

**Transient-hotel occupant,
New York City, 1978**

There are many things wrong with this analysis, as I have pointed out on other occasions, the most important being that the sixties never did throw money at problems. As the Joint Economic Committee reported in 1976, federal expenditures as a percentage of full-employment GNP have fluctuated around the 20 percent mark since the early fifties (they had reached 50 percent during World War II). So there was no quantum leap in government outlays in the sixties. To be sure, a certain shift did occur: the defense component declined, social expenditures went up. But fully two-thirds of that new civilian spending was concentrated in two programs, Medicare and increased social security benefits for the aging. These were hardly radical measures. The social security increments were, among other things, a confession of the fact that the program had been so inadequately funded that millions of the elderly were living below the poverty line (and after the raises, millions still are). Medicare was a tardy, and only partial, installment on a national health system which America, alone among the industrial democracies, does not have. **A**nd yet the impression persisted that Nixon was quite right. His theory had enormous resonance and persuaded some liberal Democratic politicians to make an abrupt change in course. When people *think* that the sixties spent wildly, that is almost as much of a political fact as if the sixties had actually done so. But why this illusion? In part because the Johnson administration often talked as if it were re-creating the world every morning. Its programs, Daniel Patrick Moynihan was to remark in retrospect, were "oversold and underfinanced." The citizenry did not know that. It was convinced by the soaring rhetoric of the sixties that the United States had indeed committed itself to a major restructuring and when, at decade's end, life seemed sour, they understandably assumed that it was the failure of the grand design that caused their discontent.

Another factor that was at work promoting this disillusionment is more complex. Laissez-faire capitalism, ruled by the "invisible hand" of Adam Smith's market, did not last very long. It existed mainly in England in the nineteenth century. Capitalism in countries like France, Germany and Japan was *dirigiste* from the very outset. Then in the 1890s, the entire capitalist world solved a two-decade crisis by structural changes. The economy of competing entrepreneurs vanished; the corporations, the trusts, the cartels, appeared. So did the welfare state, first under Bismarck in Germany, then under Lloyd George in Britain. On this last count, the United States lagged far behind Europe. It took the shock of the Great Depression, the worst crisis capitalism had ever known, to prod Washington into an interventionist role in the economy. Even so, the theory behind that intervention was relatively conservative. The corporate infrastructure was, it was said, basically sound. The government needed only manipulate fiscal and monetary policy to create the conditions under which the private sector could continue to play the predominant role in the society. **T**he civil rights movement marked a critical turning point in this process. At first, it was focused on injustices so outrageous and obvious that it could marshal the support of the entire nation. The black activists of the late fifties and early sixties were nonviolent, middle-class in their manners and determined to win the most basic of rights, like the vote and access to public accommodations. But when that effort triumphed—in the federal legislation of 1964 and 1965—the movement learned a new truth: the abolition of the *de jure* humiliations of legal Jim Crow had not touched

58

Clinton, Louisiana, 1964

Birmingham, Alabama, 1963

Bronx, New York, 1963

the *de facto* discrimination of a people locked into the lowest levels of the economy. So black Americans demanded, and sometimes won, government intervention into the marketplace and the schools and the professions to redress these grievances. **A**t decade's end, similar claims were made by the women's movement. Suddenly, other groups—most notably, white working-class communities with ethnic identities whose neighborhoods bordered on the blacks'—began to borrow the methods of civil rights protest in order to fight what they thought was a new favoritism, a reverse discrimination, on behalf of the blacks. In fact, none of the government statistics shows a significant shift in the relative position of blacks in the society. But the ethnics thought that had happened. **A**t this point, a paradox emerges. It had been the genius of laissez-faire theory to rationalize inequality on the basis of impersonal laws. It was the very nature of economic reality which was said to require that those at the bottom toil and suffer as they did. A misguided sentimentalism which sought to abolish these inequities would bring ruin upon the entire system. Great masses of the people were convinced by this functional argument on behalf of inequality, or at least by bits and scraps of it. And insofar as they did, that held down their anger. One might lament the bad luck of injustice, much as one might curse a thunderstorm. But there was no point in going into the streets about it. **T**hen two things happened. Some people did go into the streets, and it was widely thought that they achieved results. So everyone went into the streets. More broadly, the society ran into the problem of "positional competition" (I borrow from the late Fred Hirsch). Economic growth could create more goods for everyone, even if they were maldistributed. But it could not make everyone first, or

New York City, 1969

even privileged. Put another way, by the time the working people got automobiles, congestion and parking problems had robbed their acquisition of the luxury aspects that the upper and middle classes had enjoyed. So a race for status, and not just wealth, began and education was seen as the key. In the past generation, it was noted that most middle-class people had college degrees and most working-class people did not. So the concept of mass higher education sent hordes of young people to college on the assumption that they would thereby become middle class. In fact, the main result was to bid up the educational "credential" required to hold a job.

In short, the individualistic ethos was breaking down, leaving people frustrated and forcing them to demand social intervention to validate their personal claims. Throughout the Western world, there was a revival of nationalist emotions— among the Welsh, the Scots, the Irish, the Québécois, the Walloons, the Catalonians, the Basques, the Bretons, the Flemish and countless other groups. But the resurgent national emotions were now focused on a new object: gaining economic and social justice, getting a fair share, influencing the workings of the visible hand of the welfare state.

As a result, the methodology of the ultra-Left prevailed even on the Right. Every group defined itself in terms of its "power"— i.e., its ability to win better treatment from the government. In the United States, there was black power and white power, Irish power, Italian power, women's power, native American power and so on. The welfare state, an advanced form of social organization, had effectively sponsored a revival of tribalism. That had many consequences, most of them too intricate to treat here. What is relevant to this chapter is that a cynical version of politics was accepted by almost everyone. Justice was out; what you could get for

Newark, New Jersey, 1972

yourself, or your group, was in. **B**ut note the paradox implicit in this point. A people disillusioned with, even angry about, politics was forced to become more political. In part, this was a defensive move, a struggle against all the "thems" who suddenly appealed as claimants for the favor of the government. In part, it was more complex than that. The specific events of the sixties and the seventies had disenchanted people about politics in general, but that did not banish medical bills, unemployment or the disastrous decline in housing available to most people. So the polls of the seventies showed that the very same people who were opposed to Washington's intervention as a general principle favored it in almost every particular. There were majorities for national health, government as a last-resort employer and so on. The building trades, often the most conservative wing of the labor movement, even favored governmental allocation of credit—a socialist demand. **S**o people lost faith in and recognized the urgent necessity of politics at the same time. It was a typical contradiction of the seventies.

Religion was in crisis, too. The traditional questions remained, but the traditional answers began to disappear.

Religion is many things. It can be one of the chief integrating mechanisms of society, a prop of the status quo; and it can be a source of subversion, like primitive Christianity or the utopian movements of late feudalism. In this analysis, I focus on one aspect of this complex: religion as the metaphysics of the masses. It identifies a hidden coherence in the implacable, indifferent and often brutal flow of life; it allows people to cope with the suffering and evil and chaos in which they live. And it does so not by means of abstractions accessible

Walter Hoving, New York City, 1978

only to the learned, but by way of symbols that speak even to the illiterate. **G**iven this definition, it is obvious that I am concerned with religion in terms of its function rather than its truth. And it is also clear that a weakening of this institution would have both societal and intimate consequences for great masses of people. **G**od, of course, has been dying for a century at least. In saying this, I make no theological judgment about the existence or nonexistence of God. I describe a social fact: that the influence of the deity in the lives of Western peoples, including those of the United States, is on the wane, and has been for some time. More to the point of this analysis, I argue that this fact, which dates from the nineteenth century at least, became particularly effective in the sixties and seventies. Here, too, the long-run trend became the short-run reality. **B**etween 1957 and 1968, the Gallup poll asked on occasion: "At the present time, do you think religion as a whole is increasing its influence on American life or losing its influence?" In April 1957, 69 percent thought it was increasing, 14 percent that it was losing, 10 percent that it was stable. The Catholics in the sample were even more positive than the other groups: 79 percent thought religion increasing in influence, a mere 7 percent thought that it was losing, and 8 percent saw no change. In 1968, only eleven years later, Gallup found an enormous shift. Now 67 percent of the national sample, and 61 percent of the Catholics, thought religion was declining; 19 percent, and 24 percent of the Catholics, that it was gaining ground; and 8 percent in both categories that it was marking time.

There had been, roughly, a fivefold increase in the number of people in the polls who saw religion losing its hold over the nation's life, and almost a ninefold increase in Catholics

New York City, 1973

taking that view. This latter figure is especially significant since Catholicism represented the largest orthodox denomination of the fifties. A startling reversal in an institution that had seemed serene and imperturbable is quite compelling. Moreover, there is independent evidence that the Gallup percentages did not register the truly seismic upheaval that was taking place within the Church. In the study made under Andrew Greeley's direction, *Catholic Schools in a Declining Church*, a 1963 survey on the attitudes of Catholics toward their church was rerun in 1973. The results were even more dramatic than those reported by Gallup. "In terms of personal faith, only 38 percent say that they feel 'very sure' when they speak to their children about religious beliefs and values. In 1973, 27 percent of the Catholics thought it was 'certainly true' that God would punish evil for all eternity, a decline of 25 percentage points in the last decade." And: "There is no way to escape the conclusion that the image of the priesthood has slipped dramatically in the last ten years. Catholics still like their priests, but they don't seem to respect them nearly as much as they did." The shifts in attitude affected conduct. In 1963, 71 percent of Catholics said that they attended mass regularly every week; in 1973, 50 percent. Monthly confession fell from 30 percent to 17 percent. But perhaps the most striking figures have to do with apostasy. Between 1967 and 1973, the rate of defections from the Church rose rapidly, particularly among the educated elite. By 1973, almost one-quarter of the Catholics who had attended college had renounced their faith. So it is that when Greeley and his associates worked out possible scenarios for 1989, their "best case"—the one most hopeful from a Catholic point of view—projected a church attendance at a level 16 percent below that in 1963; in the "worst case," only one-

New York City, 1977

third of Catholics will go to mass every week. **G**reeley and his colleagues have an analysis of why this shift took place. It was not, they say, because of the innovations of the Second Vatican Council. These, they found, were quite popular and had a positive influence on Catholics, making them more loyal to the Church, not less. But the council's impact was completely offset by Pope Paul's encyclical of 1968, *Humanae Vitae*. That document had reaffirmed Rome's traditional opposition to any form of birth control, and it appeared at a time when the majority of Catholics had decided that the birth-control pill did not offend God's law as they understood it. They had come to that conclusion, in part at least, because it seemed that the entire Church was moving in that direction. But then the clerical politicians at the Vatican decided to ignore the sentiments of the laity, of many of the priests and theologians and even of some bishops. Now *Humanae Vitae* forced Catholics to choose between their own conscientious perception that the Pill was licit and the authority of a Church that told them it was not. The issue, of course, was far from abstract. It had to do with the actual sex lives of the people concerned with it. **T**herefore, Greeley and his associates concluded, the most important single factor explaining the dramatic shift in Catholic attitudes between 1963 and 1973 was the birth-control question as it was focused by *Humanae Vitae*. As an explanation of the proximate cause of the decline in Catholic faith in the late sixties and early seventies, this theory has much to recommend it (even so, I have my reservations, which are not relevant here). What is omitted is the historic setting that made it possible for that proximate cause to have such a devastating impact. The papacy, after all, has committed more than its share of stupidities over the past century or so, but they did not cause

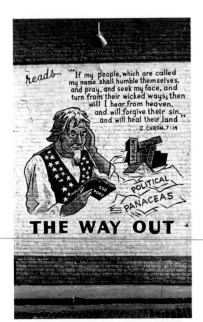

Sumter, South Carolina, 1975

mass defections from the faith, particularly in the United States, traditionally the most orthodox of Catholic populations. This mistake had tremendous effect. Why? **B**ecause in this instance, as in so many others during the past decade, the long-run and the short-run contradictions merged. It is a cliché of Western social thought that this society has been in the process of secularization under the impact of science and technology for well over a century. The world, Max Weber said so brilliantly, is being *"entzäubert"*—demystified. And Hans Küng, the author of one of the most influential pro-Catholic books of the seventies, acknowledges that man has "taken under his control much—indeed almost everything—for which God, superhuman and supermundane powers and spirits were supposed to be responsible." However, true as the cliché is, it has to be rescued from its banality if it is to be of any help in illuminating complex relationships.

Knoxville, Tennessee, 1981

It is obvious enough that the triumph of Western rationality has severely limited the areas of human experience that require— or can tolerate—the existence of God as a working hypothesis. Meteorologists, rather than divine whims, now explain the weather. Even Greeley, who does not like many of the conclusions that are usually derived from this proposition, conceded its validity while trying to limit it. As a result, the churches tended to become, in Paul Valéry's phrase, "no longer sacred, or else nothing but sacred." Therefore, when a *Humanae Vitae* appears, a cultural process that has been going on for generations allows the event to make deep fissures within an established, but weakened faith.

True enough, Greeley says in his book *Unsecular Man*. But science, he argues, cannot answer the religious questions about the meaning of life and death. I think that is quite right. Therefore, Greeley continues, religion must remain as a powerful force. That is not necessarily true at all, and certainly not true in the seventies. We could be entering a new phase in the history of Western humanity (I make this parochial restriction because of my ignorance of non-Western civilizations), in which there will indeed be religious questions—but no effective religious answers. That unsettling possibility has been glimpsed more clearly in the seventies, I would suggest, than in any preceding era. Greeley himself accurately describes the spiritual reality: "many young people have nothing to believe in, no interpretative scheme, have no mythology which will give order, coherence, purpose to their lives . . . . They do not know why they are, where they are going, or why they live." **T**his crisis announces itself to the individual conscience; yet it obviously has enormous social ramifications, even if they are more complicated than the secularization cliché sometimes implies. In one conventional analysis, religion is a symbolic integration of a community, its transcendent self in palpable form. It is, Hegel said, the "ethical substance" which permeates the consciousness of individuals and provides them with instinctive truths and norms. Religion, Durkheim remarked, always really worships society. **B**ut what about the tremendous growth of fundamentalist and ecstatic religions in the United States in recent years? Max Weber provided the basis for answering that question long ago. The more scientific and calculated culture becomes, he said, the more religion is forced into the sphere of the irrational. "On the one side, there is a rational knowledge and domination of nature, on the other, 'mystical' experiences whose unutterable content is the one possible form of the divine in a mechanistic world from which God has been removed." Later on, Leszek Kolakowski deepened that

Zen Buddhist monastery, Rochester, New York, 1979

Zen Buddhist monastery, Rochester, New York, 1979

insight: "A rain of gods is falling from the sky on the funeral of the one God who has outlived himself. The atheists have their saints and the blasphemers are erecting chapels."

Kolakowski's last sentence should give old-fashioned atheists pause. God's death, he is saying, makes people so lonely that they invent new faiths, some of them the work of antibelievers. For instance, there were forms of group therapy in the seventies which struck me as attempts to willfully re-create the superego which no longer broods in our psyches. Primitive magic returns, masquerading as science. These cults, as well as the revival of fundamentalism, were, and are, desperate attempts to disguise the earthly void which reflects the empty heavens. **S**o the seventies was the decade in which a centuries-old secularization trend finally became a commonplace. That clearly could contribute to the bewilderment of a society. Not so obviously, it might even have broader economic and social effects. Western capitalism, as Fred Hirsch pointed out in *Social Limits to Growth*, has always depended on precapitalist virtues. People, Adam Smith said, "could safely be trusted to pursue their self-interest without undue harm to the community not only because of the restrictions imposed by the law, but also because they were subject to built-in restraint derived from morals, religion, custom and education." **N**ow society has become larger and more complex than Smith could have ever imagined. More and more people are not neighbors within communities, but individuals within an anonymous world of masses. To take a simple, homely example: there are no friends to frown on you when you litter on the sidewalks of a gigantic city or of a suburban shopping center. So why refrain from littering? Or from other forms of antisocial behavior which are not monitored by either police or peers? In particular, why should you limit yourself when the official ideology tells you that your own enjoyment is the supreme good? In short, the industrial democracies have a practical need for norms and self-restraint—at a time when the traditional supports of norms and self-restraint are being destroyed. **I**n his study *The Cultural Contradictions of Capitalism*, Daniel Bell considers some of these matters and then asks: "Can we—must we not—re-establish that which is sacred and that which is profane?" I wish we could. I do not think we can. **T**he essence of a traditional religion, an Arab thinker once remarked, is that its devotees do not know that it is traditional. Put another way, society cannot deliberately create a spontaneous faith just because it senses that void within itself. Faith is either there or it isn't; but it cannot be willed into being. "The unwritten and unerring laws of the gods," Sophocles wrote, "did not come into being today or yesterday. They are always there and no one knows whence they come." If you seek after the origins of those laws, Hegel added, they have already lost their validity.

On the Fourth of July 1976, I was deeply moved as I watched the tall ships advance in stately procession up the Hudson River. It was an appropriate drama for a visionary nation which had inscribed on its Great Seal, "New Order of the Ages." Only, I observed the event from the thirty-fifth-floor roof of the apartment house into which I had just moved, and my wife and I did not know anyone there except the hired staff. New York is, of course, the site of the loneliest of the American crowds and perhaps I am not fair. Or is it? Los Angeles, that vast complex of freeways, is also an enormous conglomeration of strangers, shoulder to shoulder at fifty-five miles an hour.

Queens, New York, 1965

Or there was the jubilee in London for the twenty-fifth anniversary of Queen Elizabeth's coronation. I am against royalty, a committed republican, yet one would be a fool to ignore the genuine need that those rites fulfilled. Yet they are an anachronism. Charming and graceful and historical as a royal family may be, it can hardly be the center of a modern society. Like the tall ships, it can give grandeur to a day or two among a people hungry for some palpable sign of their collective transcendence, for some larger meaning. But that is all: a day or two. **B**ut where, then, will we find the sacraments of society, the outward signs of our inward grace? And more to the point, where will we find the inward grace? Up until now that has been a given. Can it be taken?

It is dangerous to answer yes. The totalitarian potential of public religion was implicit in Rousseau's formulation of the ideas in *The Social Contract.* The sovereign, he said, had the right to determine "a purely civil creed," "not precisely as dogmas of religion, but as sentiments of sociability without which it is impossible to be a good citizen or a loyal subject." And he immediately added: "Though unable to oblige anyone to believe in them, the sovereign can banish from the state anyone who does not." More largely, if society itself explicitly becomes the successor of God, does that not give it infinite powers which it has only finite ability to exercise?

In the 1980 elections yet another dangerous solution to this problem emerged. The politicized Christian fundamentalists proposed, in the name of "conservatism," to use government to impose their sectarian definitions of morality on the 80 percent or so of the population which did not share them. The demons of pornography, abortion, homosexuality and humanism were to be exorcised by the same federal power which was held to be the very source of all evil. The last time that happened was both a fiasco and much worse: Prohibition, which gave such an enormous impetus to the rise of organized crime in the United States. The new attempt to legislate goodness will fail just as Prohibition did—but the costs in human freedom and public liberty might be even greater. This is the treacherous ground on which we ventured, without knowing it, in the seventies. We have no choice but to grope toward something that has never existed before, an agnostic civilization. There will, of course, be people within it who believe in God, but God, for the economic and sociological and cultural reasons already given, cannot symbolize its unity.

But why believe that such a radical undertaking is remotely possible? And this question is particularly pointed when one remembers I have already conceded that a reaction (not the only one) to the bewilderments of the seventies has been a turn toward conservatism. I make these proposals because I am certain that conservatism will not work. The retreat into pre-Keynesian economics—visible in both the Nixon-Ford and Carter administrations—the social meanness and massive subsidies for the rich of Ronald Reagan will not cope with the problems of the economy any more than fundamentalist fervor will restore God to the central place He once occupied in the common consciousness of Western humanity. Either we will find democratic, humane ways of dealing with these crises or else the future will be subjected to terrible simplifications, most likely imposed on it by some authoritarian, or totalitarian, bureaucracy. And strangely enough, I see reason for hope in the very pervasiveness of the sense of decline. In

Washington, D.C., 1978

the mid-seventies, two sociologists at Columbia University, Amitai Etzioni and Thomas DiPrete, discussed the various polls showing the fall of popular confidence in the major American institutions. Each institution, they noted, had agonized over its own lack of popularity and sought ways to counter it. But what each did not realize is that they were part of a generalized lack of trust in all institutions. "Since it stands to reason that a problem common to all institutions cannot be remedied in any one alone, what is required of reformers is greater attention to the underlying societal structure."

The very ubiquity of our social confusions, then, might be reason for hope—because eventually it might force us to look for more radical transformations rather than seek shelter in an impossible conservatism. This is not to argue on behalf of a catastrophic optimism in which chaos must give birth to a star. Our chaos could give birth to more chaos. I simply but emphatically hold that there is a resilience and creativity in this land and that we might—just might—act out of a reasoned desperation born of so many simultaneous disillusionments. If that is to happen, we must be aware that it is a possibility. The second half of this book concerns the rise that might be made possible by the decline I have just described. It deals not with its probability, but only with its possibility. It is an attempt to say *sotto voce* that we just might be able to begin to master these forces that now overmaster us.

RISE?

Could all these disintegrations be the prelude to hope? Does the time of in-between portend not decline and fall, but decline and rise? Perhaps. **I** have a number of problems in even suggesting this possibility. One of them is analogous to Milton's difficulties with Satan. In his epic poem the prince of darkness was a much more fascinating figure than the God of light. So today, it is much easier to describe fragmentation and bewilderment, which are the palpable, familiar facts of daily life, than to imagine a new and healthy wholeness. Almost twenty years ago, in *The Accidental Century*, I wrote of modernist culture as a "magnificent decadence," arguing that the breakdown of social, moral and aesthetic norms had provided a few uprooted geniuses like Joyce, Mann and Proust with an incomparable subject matter. But when those writers tried to describe what they were for, they became, at best, ambiguous. Molly Bloom's sexual surrender with its rapturous "yeses" is preceded by the comment, "and I thought well as well him as another"; Hans Castorp simply disappears into World War I; Marcel rediscovers the tea and madeleine.

Now I face a similar difficulty, only it is political, not artistic. I can describe what is wrong in terms of personal experiences, statistics and trends; I know the details of this age but I only suspect the existence of its angels (or, more prosaically, of men and women capable of making a new beginning in the ruins of our culture). That problem is compounded by the fact that I am an aging prophet without honor. My hopes for a rational and democratic resolution of our crises contradict the dominant mood—the certain, existential knowledge which requires no proof—of these times. Everyone "knows" that the sixties failed and that the eighties must retreat before the antisocial facts of life. These things are now as certain as the conviction in the fifties that there was no poverty in the affluent society. **B**ut when I was a prophet without honor in that earlier period, I was also immortal. I was in my twenties and early thirties and there was world enough and time in which to be proved right, and it was quite pleasant on the margin of the society waiting for people to come to their senses. That youthful confidence was, *mirabile dictu*, rewarded. In the sixties, I became a prophet with honor in my own country as my preposterous vision of the poverty in the other America became a cliché for cocktail parties and final exams.

Now I am a prophet without honor again, which is a familiar, even comfortable, role for me. Only this time I am in my early fifties. I am no less persuaded by my critique of the established—mean—wisdom than I was two decades ago. Only I am more anxious and impatient and I am conscious of time's winged chariot. And perhaps it is not well to be looking back over one's shoulder when talking of the future, to have lost the serenity of one's dissatisfaction with the present.

All of this should not be taken to mean that I doubt that decline may end in rise. Even the elections of 1980 did not cause me to do that. Indeed, as I noted at the very beginning of this book, I even found some confirmation of my insights in Ronald Reagan's rhetoric during that campaign. That analytic convergence of Left and Right has happened before.

Nineteenth-century aristocrats and workers in England often attacked the emerging bourgeois order on the same grounds but for utterly different purposes (the aristocrats wanted to go back to feudalism, the workers to go forward to socialism). Indeed when Marx wrote his magnificent description of the way in which capitalism corrupts all idyllic values in the *Communist Manifesto* he was talking about the same transformations which so horrified the proto-conservative Edmund Burke in his *Reflections on the French Revolution*. And Marx prized the descriptions of bourgeois society by Balzac, a committed reactionary, more than the account of the same process in the novels of the socialist Émile Zola. So the difference between Left and Right on the disintegration of the old order is not, or at least not necessarily, a matter of depicting it or even of evaluating its destructive force. Having arrived at common conclusions with regard to the problem, the conservatives advocate the politics of nostalgia, the radicals look toward a new future. That is, the Right urges an impossible illusion, the Left a problematic possibility. I have no difficulty in choosing between such options even in a time when the cultural mood prefers illusions to possibility. More to the present point, the conservative dreams will, sooner rather than later, dissolve and turn into their contrary.

I was reinforced in my socialist convictions on these matters some months before the 1980 Republican convention by Milton Friedman. The occasion was the taping of a discussion with that eminent conservative, which was appended to the first installment of his televised panegyric to the glories of the free market. Pointing to all of the subsidies demanded and received by the corporations, I commented that big business did not really want the government out of the economy, as Friedman proposed, but rather merely wanted to subordinate

Washington's intervention to corporate purpose. You're absolutely right, Friedman said (I paraphrase from memory, but fairly). The businessmen are about as bad as your intellectuals. That was amusing and even gracious; it was also a forthright declaration of political bankruptcy. Friedman was admitting that his intricate supply-and-demand curves intersect in the abstract space of a totally free market and have nothing to do with contemporary capitalist reality. **I**ndeed, that was why Ronald Reagan had to contradict himself in the 1980 campaign. He simultaneously advocated Friedman-esque restraint on the part of the government *and* a regressive tax cut which invoked the name of John Kennedy but was much more ultra-Keynesian than Kennedy had ever dared be. That is, the Republican candidate mixed an ancient, Adam Smithian and a recent, John Kennedyesque nostalgia. At least one conservative, the columnist George Will, understood the resultant contradiction. The Republicans, he commented, had come up with two themes. "One is cultural conservatism. The other is capitalist dynamism." Only "the latter dissolves the former." **M**y opponents on the right, then, strengthen me in my Leftist heresies. They recognize the same crises that I do, yet the future they project is a past that never worked. To be sure, their economic fairy tales have the real-world function of rationalizing government acquiescence in the corporate agenda and their illusions impose hardships on flesh-and-blood people. But reality will have its revenge sooner or later, and my ideas will once again become at least possible (which is as good as things ever get in politics). I do not, however, propose to wait around for History to vindicate my prophecies now without honor. And for all the Miltonic problems of imagining a decent society, one has to try to say what you are for. I will angle toward my

The Fashion Center, Paramus, New Jersey, 1981

imagined future by way of a rehabilitation of the immediate past, arguing that things could be much better than they now are because, contrary to the assumption that reforms always fail and cause more harm than good, the present is better than the past. A personal tragedy, an infuriatingly partial victory and an amusement park are my evidence.

My mother began to die in the spring of 1978. A vibrant, active woman who had been deeply involved in civic causes and had traveled the world, she was destroyed, inch by inch, over a period of two years. It was as if she had fallen into the hands of some fascist dictator bent on torturing her to death. The last seven or eight months, she was in a nursing home, the best I could find, a good and kindly place, yet a gentle bedlam of men and women living out what had become a sentence of life. The last time I saw her, about two weeks before the end, she knew me, but that was about all. When the phone rang at six in the morning in late July 1980 and I learned that she had been found dead in her bed at the hospital, my first reaction was one of relief, of happiness that the degradation and humiliation were over for her. **I** go into these brief, horrible details so that I am not misunderstood. Politics cannot triumph over death or aging. All it can do is to change the circumstances in which the tragic limitations of the human condition assert themselves. Laws can ameliorate the economic and social causes and consequences of those limitations, but not the limitations themselves. So I have long thought that, my friend Karl Marx to the contrary notwithstanding, a just society might be more religious, not less, because then people would suffer not from the injustices of the distribution of wealth or medical services, but from their

**Retiree, Westport,
New York, 1978**

"When my father grew old, the children took care of him. If there were no social security, the church would have to take care of me."

86

Retiree, DuQuoin, Illinois, 1976

own inescapable mortality. And yet. **I**f there was no social security or Medicare, my mother's protracted death—and the more sudden going of my mother-in-law some five weeks earlier—would have disrupted, and perhaps destroyed, my own family. Over those two years of incremental agony, the hospital bills totaled tens of thousands of dollars; so did the seven weeks of care which preceded my mother-in-law's death. Though there is no law in the world which could have protected those two women from the ravages of their essential humanity, the existing laws at least freed them and their families from an economic fate almost as cruel as the physical assault upon their bodies. **T**he political change in the nature of age and death began in the 1930s when Dr. Francis Townsend, a California doctor who had been influenced by the socialist movement in his youth, saw three elderly women picking through his garbage, looking for food. As a result of that epiphany, he organized a movement of the aging which was not always wise—it made some alliances with Rightist demagogues on occasion—but which was a factor in winning the Social Security Act, the very centerpiece of the American welfare state (it, Medicare and other federal retirement programs account for about two-thirds of all social spending). There are, to be sure, enormous imperfections, structural problems even, in this system. As the crises of stagflation developed in the seventies and early eighties, high rates of unemployment reduced the amount of money paid into social security and soaring prices increased the costs of the benefits which were paid out. And there is talk of "capping" the regular rise in social security payments which results from automatically adjusting them upward along with the consumer price index. **L**et there be no doubt: progress can

**Elderly communalists,
Evanston, Illinois, 1976**

unravel, it is not inevitable, and America could decide to make aging and death more socially and economically vicious than they are now. But let there also be no mistake: it is better to be over sixty-five in America today than in 1934, before social security, or 1964, before Medicare. The major American reform program has worked, not failed, and there is thus no eternal, neoconservative law which says that all governmentally induced social change is bad. Moreover, and this is another reason for the optimism which I derive from the tragedy in which I was an involved and helpless spectator, there is a political movement which might be able to hold back any attempts to march the society backward in this area. I spoke at the Western Gerontological Society meeting in Denver in March 1977. There were several thousand people in attendance, about half of them over sixty-five, the others made up of professionals and students in the field. I learned more than I taught. It was not so much a matter of the ideas I heard, though they were obviously important, too. It was after I spoke, when the floor opened up for discussion and people lined up at the microphones, that I suddenly realized I was sitting in the middle of a social movement. There was the eagerness and the anger, the internal quarrels and the intent listening that I had encountered in the civil rights movement of the fifties and sixties, in antipoverty campaigns and the fight against the war in Vietnam. There was hope. It was the time of the political battle to end the compulsory retirement laws and the people in Denver understood that their "gray power" was making a difference. There was fear. A doctor from the Northwest told of how people with treatable illnesses were diagnosed as "senile" and left to deteriorate into an unnecessarily bitter and even early death. There were, he said, abundant moneys for cheap drug thera-

After fishing, Wilcox County, Alabama, 1966

pies which could dope the aging into a passive acceptance of their fate. Yet there were not enough funds for truly rehabilitative therapies. As that doctor was speaking, there was a murmur of outraged assent from the older people in the audience. It was clear that, within the limits imposed on them by their bodies, their spirits were militant. **T**hese encounters, personal and political, with the aging made me—make me—hopeful that this time of disintegration is prelude to a period of new departures. So did a trip to the South in the summer of 1977, when I faced up to the enormous, and frustratingly limited, gains made by the civil rights movement, which I had participated in from 1954 to 1968.

My wife, Stephanie, our two children, Alexander and Teddy, and I left New York in a rented station wagon heading toward Florida in July 1977. I hoped that the kids would get a sense of their country. The ambiguities asserted themselves at the very outset. We crossed the Hudson and drove across the New Jersey flats, an industrial moonscape built on swampland, a desolate stretch of looming factories and chemically polluted water. Then one passes a futuristic scene of huge, continuous-process plants, labyrinths of steel pipe without a single human being visible to the eye. I loathed these sights— and then almost immediately accused myself of an aesthetic fallacy. For working people, these grim and graceless buildings are as much the means of life as a lovely undulating field of wheat, and if the choice is between alienating work in a degraded environment and no work at all, I, like them, am for the former. I want new, more human, choices, of course; so do they. But how to get them? **W**e drove south and

Oil refinery, Bayonne, New Jersey, 1981

reached the Outer Banks, the island slivers off the North Carolina coast where the American land ends. We had hoped for an unsullied beauty; when we approached Kitty Hawk we found a near Coney Island of wall-to-wall motels and beach houses. There were fast-food places perched on the ocean, serving frozen fish imported from Iceland. There was one exception to this dreary rule, a restaurant at Ocrakoke that served the day's catch while you looked out on the fishing boats which had brought it in. But in general, we found a thousand miles of franchised, homogenized, not very tasteful food and very little seafood to be had on the very edge of the teeming ocean. **I** could go on with the paradoxes and ambiguities, for the time of in-between is pregnant with many contraries. But the event which really made me think took place in a Holiday Inn on the North Carolina mainland and it had to do with race in the United States. **H**oliday Inns are one of the few products of American capitalism that I like, more or less. They are, of course, utterly predictable and stereotyped but their standardized mediocrity at least establishes a lower limit which is important to someone like me who spends a good portion of the year on the road. They are, to hazard an unscientific and random observation, key institutions of the working-class vacation in this country and in the late afternoon their swimming pools turn into a kind of community center for children who have never known one another before and never will again. We stayed in them from New York to Florida and it was in that Holiday Inn in North Carolina that an insight about race relations in America— above all, in the South—came into focus. **I** had begun to notice the phenomenon in Maryland when we passed public pools where whites and blacks were swimming together. I

Married couple, Atlanta, Georgia, 1980

Cairo, Illinois, 1978

thought back to the bitter struggles on the Lake Michigan shore in Chicago, where the attempted integration of a beach led to a bloody riot. A civil rights strategist told me then that the last two places in the world where blacks and whites would come together were bars (because of the danger of drunken violence) and pools (because of the sexual charge associated with half-naked bodies). But along the road in Maryland we saw that the impossible had happened and even become commonplace. **S**till, the revelation really came in that Holiday Inn in North Carolina. The sight was simple enough: in the coffee shop in the morning, a white waitress served a grizzled, old black man in workclothes. That was all. Yet I found it difficult to hold back my tears while I tried to explain what was happening to Alex and Teddy. **I** grew up in Saint Louis, a border city with *de facto* segregation. I was sixteen and a college student in Massachusetts before I sat in a movie theater with blacks. The first time I went south as a conscious integrationist adult was in 1956. I was there to discuss a prize which a liberal foundation, the Fund for the Republic, was bestowing on a woman editor in Mississippi. The honoree was terrified because of the honor and begged me to award it to someone else (for legal reasons, we couldn't do that even if we wanted to). More to the point, when we lunched in a hotel dining room in Jackson, we agreed that if anyone recognized her, I would be introduced as her insurance agent. **L**ater, the drama and incipient violence of the Southern hostility to integration became much more pronounced. When I attended the second meeting of the Student Nonviolent Coordinating Committee in Atlanta in the fall of 1960, some racists drove at night through the college campus where we were assembled. In 1964, I arrived in Mississippi

"Nigger, nigger, nigger"
—resident of a predominantly
black neighborhood.

New York City, 1968

Birmingham, Alabama, 1963

Democratic National Convention, Atlantic City, New Jersey, 1964

for a week's stay just as the murderers of three civil rights workers were arrested. I felt like a member of an underground in my own country. I drove with absolute regard for the traffic laws since I did not want to meet any sheriff unnecessarily. Was it mere paranoia that when I phoned my wife I spoke to her in French?

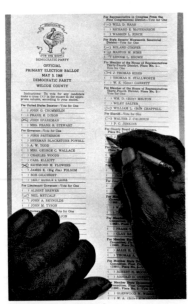

First voter, Camden, Alabama, 1966

I marched down the eerie, empty streets of Montgomery with Martin Luther King in 1965 when the only people visible were the soldiers of the federalized national guard—sullen Southerners acting under court order—protecting our right to assemble. Three years later I walked down the same empty streets in Memphis to a union rally in memory of the slain Martin Luther King. Now, in 1977, that surging, singing movement which King had led so magnificently was gone, but the white waitress was serving the black man his breakfast. Here was a scene that would have been impossible fifteen years before—or that might have provoked a riot. So it seemed to me that I had discovered a simple, unambiguous fact, a justification for my hope that the decadences I saw all around me were the preparation for a new beginning. I should have known that my emotional reaction was simplistic. Shortly after that trip south, I was talking to a correspondent for a European magazine about that moment in North Carolina. She had spent ten years in the United States and she listened to my optimistic account and replied: You mean that it took that gigantic movement with all of those confrontations and risks and tragedies and that all you accomplished was the right to a cup of coffee and the vote? Did nothing more basic change? I knew, and wrote about, the economic and social limits of black political gains even while the movement was in full swing. And Martin Luther King, with whom I discussed these matters, knew

"I Have a Dream" speech, Martin Luther King, March on Washington, 1963

Sheriff Arnold, Wilcox County, Alabama, 1980

them better than I. No doubt that some of the brightest and most talented of the black young rose up on the income and occupation ladder during the sixties and seventies. But during all those years black unemployment was, and still is, double that of whites, and unemployment of black youth has been a plague, the breeding ground for addicts and muggers and alcoholics. Even demographics are against the minorities: in the mid-eighties, the whites will experience a "baby bust" and it will be easier for the young to find jobs, but the blacks will continue to grow in numbers and little will change unless American politics turns a sharp corner. **I**ndeed, it seemed to me in 1980 that the Miami riots were the psychological opposite of the urban violence of the second half of the sixties. The explosions in Watts and Detroit and Newark and the other cities were born of impatience and hope. A people which had long been denied the most fundamental rights had become conscious of itself and the resultant militancy was intended to hurry up history, which was finally moving in the right direction. To put it paradoxically, the angry blacks in the streets in the sixties were there because they believed in America and wanted the fulfillment of its promise at once. In Miami in 1980, the riot was a reaction of despair, the blind fury of a community which felt itself neglected, losing ground, beleaguered by Cubans who, for a variety of sociological and economic reasons, had made greater progress than the blacks. Miami was a rising in a dead-end street. **I**n part, these tragedies happened because of Vietnam. Until the escalation of that unconscionable war in 1965, the sixties had the promise of being the most creative decade since the thirties, and Martin Luther King and his movement were the vanguard of that possibility. But then the war shifted the focus of the society totally and King rightly went into opposition against

Since the Voting Rights Act of 1965, there are many black elected officials—and black lawmen—throughout the South.

Lyndon Johnson and others who had been his allies in some of the earlier struggles. The battles against the sectional prejudices of the South were largely won; but the fight against the structural racism of an economic system which assigns minorities and women to an inherently inferior place was defeated almost before it had begun. **S**o that black man having his coffee in the Holiday Inn in North Carolina is unimportant? Not at all. That incident cannot be taken as an excuse for not getting on with the enormous work that remains to be done in the battle against racism. But it is a testament to the efficacy of precisely what is needed in that future fight: of men and women, black and white, banding together courageously to change some of the fundamental conditions of their lives. Moreover, I am heartened by the sheer ordinariness of what I saw in North Carolina, the victory incarnated in an unimportant detail, in a cup of coffee. That is the point. One does not look forward to an integrated America in which every day is a civil rights rally but to a society in which human relations between the races are taken for granted. The fact that my sons did not understand why I was on the verge of tears is a good sign. The gains we made were too little and frustrating and so much remains to be done. But change is possible—change which is so profound that it penetrates to the minutiae of life, to the serving of breakfast in a Holiday Inn.

My third reason for hope is an amusement park, a popular, glittering superficiality called Disney World. I visited it on that trip in 1977 and before and since. I find it one of the most intriguing symbols in American society and another reason for thinking that decline might—might—lead to rise.

Cinderella's Castle, Magic Kingdom, Disney World, 1981

Main Street, Disney World, 1981

At first, it might seem absurd to take Disney World seriously. But on that trip in 1977, as I walked down the streets of a fraudulent Middle Western small town built in the middle of steaming Florida, I thought of Ernest Bloch. Bloch, a most heterodox Marxist, was remarkably sensitive to the presence of the utopian impulse in the strangest places. For him, the circus, with its exotic animals evoking mysterious, distant places, conjured up the South Sea utopia where the lion and the lamb lie down together. And the epicureanism of the masses in France, the ordinary people participating in a wine culture, and even aspects of a *haute cuisine*, was for him an anticipation of a day when everyone would enjoy what are now the pleasures of the elite. Bloch should have come to Disney World. The park exists on at least three levels. First, there is the obvious Disney World of "rides" and tugging, anxious children and harried adults. But then, second, there is in this vulgarly romantic representation of a Norman Rockwell past a testimony to something people want to believe in. The crowds lined up and waited patiently, paying a good deal of money to fantasize themselves into a society without lines or money. Was there a yearning for community in the midst of this hustling, commercial enterprise? I think so. When I went back in 1980, I was struck by the number of foreigners in pursuit of that dream, but then Hollywood has long made the towns of nineteenth-century America into a planetary myth of a simpler past. There is even an "attraction" in the park which dramatizes this global theme. It is called Small, Small World and one rides on a (grooved, guided) boat through shallow water past grottoes in which there are ridiculously chauvinist images of the variety of human culture. Every mannequin has the same Anglo-Saxon face and pert nose, only some of them are brown,

Disney World, 1981

Monorail in lobby of the Contemporary Hotel, Disney World, 1981

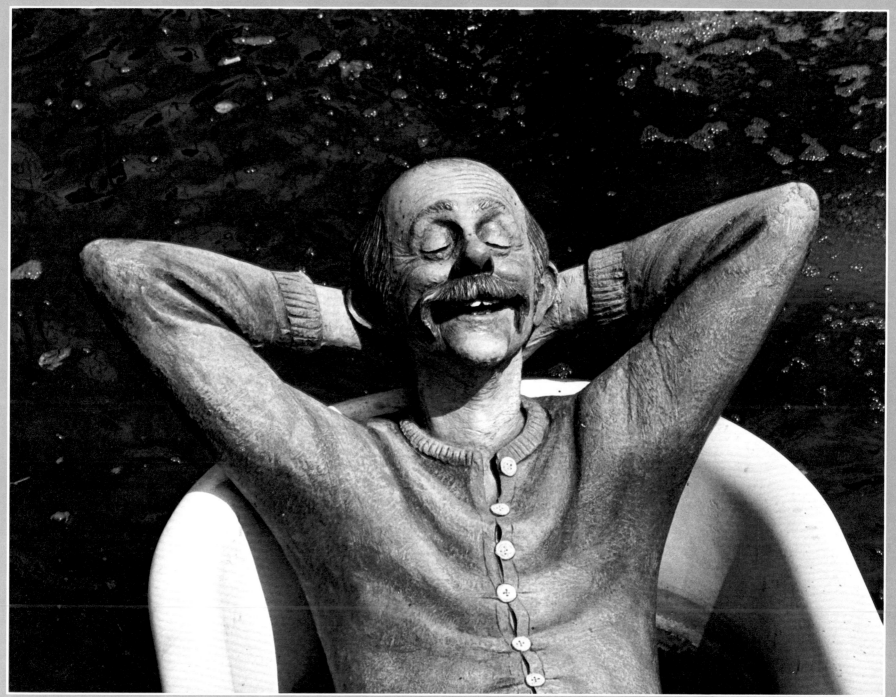

Animated plastic figure, Disney World, 1981

some yellow, some black and so on. It is a preposterous image of the unity of humankind with angelic choirs singing on Muzak all the while. And it reaches out to something deep within the people: if it is blatantly sentimental, the sentimentality is utopian. The third level of Disney World is, in part quite literally, invisible. There are no cars in the place, which is built over an intricate system of tunnels in which all of the utility pipes and lines are located in the ceiling for easy access. There is a Swedish-built waste disposal system which carries mountains of garbage by means of suction at fifty miles an hour and deposits the refuse in a plant which recycles it. Some of the water used in the park is then piped and treated by passing it through a pool of hyacinths; there is one solar building, and there have been grants from the Department of Housing and Urban Development for the "people moving" systems, which keep the attendance, and the money, flowing. In short, underneath this bogus, nostalgic America of the nonexistent past is the technology of a futuristic utopia.

Unfortunately, Walt Disney and his heirs were quite conscious of this potential. Disney came from a Debsian socialist family and became a conservative Republican (when he went to the White House to receive a medal from Lyndon Johnson in 1964, he wore a Goldwater for President pin in his lapel). He believed that his park was an Experimental Prototype Community of Tomorrow (EPCOT in Disneyspeak) and in 1982 a new section of Disney World will open up with corporate exhibits showing how the private sector will be able to solve all of our social problems with expensive, profitable technologies. Even more to the point, Disney created his park in the name of free enterprise but carefully designed it as an absolute monopoly in an area the size of Manhattan. Thus he could decide that his patrons would not be able to

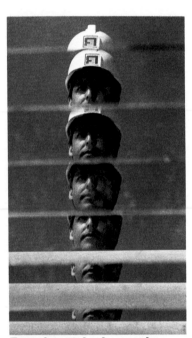

Experimental solar panels, Disney World, Florida, 1981

Tunnel, Disney World, 1981

buy chewing gum. **I**n other words, that third, and hidden, level of Disney World is not one utopia, but two, and in that fact it is more symbolic of the present and future than Disney knew. Like so many things in this society, the magnificent technology under the Magic Kingdom could be used for the creation of a bureaucratic, orderly, mesmerized society dominated by corporate planners. That is what Disney World in fact already is. But those same innovations could be the basis for the creation of environmentally decent, clean and unpolluted cities. There is a real utopia hidden underneath Cinderella's Castle in central Florida.

So there are existing reasons for hope. The welfare state is not a failure, for aging is more humane in the United States today than it was a generation ago; the civil rights movement did not even begin to subvert the economic and social structures of racism but it made palpable, even enormous, changes in American life which I saw symbolized in a cup of coffee in North Carolina; and Walt Disney, the conservative genius with a Midas touch, may have unwittingly explored some of the avenues to the Leftist future. **G**rant all the things I have just evoked. Let it be taken as proved that the social reforms of the immediate past and present are not the utter failure defined by the conservative clichés of the early eighties. Even assume that there will indeed be a next America, that this decade is a time of decision, of basic change analogous to the transformations of the New Deal. What then would that next America actually look like? And if one can overcome Milton's problem and describe the good to come as plausibly as the evil which is already here, how can one move politically toward such a future?

What the next America *should* be can be put simply enough. Let me state it as an abstraction and then explore the connotations, the images, the experiences which have led me to that conclusion and which can lend it some flesh and blood. If the United States is to cope with those multiple and intersecting crises which I described earlier, then a precondition—not a sufficient condition, but an absolute necessity—is that the investment process be democratized. By that I mean that the fundamental decisions now made by giant corporations about what to produce and where to produce it and whom to hire and what price to charge and what needs to meet must involve the actual producers, the affected communities and the political system, from the neighborhood on up to the nation as a whole and ultimately to global institutions. That would not yet be socialism, since it envisions only a partial democratization of economic power, with corporations and their private interest still paying a major role; but it would be located far beyond, and to the left, of anything in the present liberal tradition and practice.

But what do these programs and strategies have to do with the cultural crisis described at the outset of this book? Will the democratization of investment bring God back to life?

Of course not. But there is a very important insight of Hegel's which applies here. Hegel was probably the first sociologist of religion, the inspiration of Durkheim as well as of Marx. His description of Roman decadence—which was the precondition of Christian triumph—in the *Phenomenology* is haunting and poetic as well as profound. The spirit has departed the Roman religion, Hegel writes: "The statues are now corpses in stone . . . the hymns of praise are words from which all belief has gone." That happened, he said, because

Razing Chrysler's Dodge main plant, Detroit, Michigan, 1981

Roman society became totally individualistic, hedonistic. God died (and Hegel uses that phrase on a number of occasions) because the community, the solidarity, the shared values which He represented had disappeared. As Marx was to put the same idea, the earthly family is the secret of the heavenly family. **T**here is, I believe, a similar link between the economy and the spiritual crisis in the United States. The latter is not a mere projection, an epiphenomenon, of the former. As I made clear earlier on, the devaluing of values is a process which has been going on for at least a century. At the same time, however, the public bewilderments of the past decade or so, the collapse of the arrogant sixties' certitude that the economy had been tamed, the sense of a social system somehow out of control, have all reinforced those disintegrative spiritual trends. And if, in contrast, the policies described here were implemented, that would not restore a past which is dead and gone, but it might at least make possible a next America, a new basis of human solidarity and therefore of higher values. **O**ne problem in making this abstraction real is that America is the most ideological nation on the face of the earth. **T**o most citizens of this country that statement sounds preposterous. After all, it is the Europeans and then the communists and now the Third World who get entangled in all those "isms." America is the land of the pragmatists, of a people who do not theorize about machines but get them to work with a knowing kick or the rap of a wrench. But that nonideology, that anti-ideology, is itself a tenacious ideology which filters the national experience, adjusting the data to fit the (anti-ideological) conclusions. Keynes understood that brilliantly. Every tough-minded, no-nonsense practical man, he once wrote, is usually in the thrall of some outmoded book from a previous generation whose title he might not even know. When one thinks, as so many Americans do, that one is approaching reality without any assumptions, that is the most enormous, and inevitably false, assumption of them all. **C**onsider just a few bits of the recent evidence. Two of the central industries of the American economy, the very spine of the system as it were, are auto and steel. During the postwar period their managements made spectacularly inefficient investment decisions: in the case of auto, the refusal to build a small, high-mileage car, a policy which led to the loss of between 20 percent and 25 percent of the American market as well as the creation of the most wasteful energy infrastructure in the world; in the case of steel, the payment of high dividends and the use of capital to speculate in other industries rather than putting that money into the modernization of steel itself, a strategy which made the United States into a technologically backward competitor on the world market. There are elaborate rationales for these disastrous choices. The consumer, the auto industry says, made us do it—even though the United Automobile Workers told Detroit in 1949 that Americans wanted small cars and would buy them from the Europeans and the Japanese if they were not produced here. Environmental regulations, the steel executives argue, forced us to invest in (presumably unimportant) equipment to protect people from pollution—even though, as a report of the Congressional Office of Technology Assessment in 1980 documented, the Japanese had environmental costs 65 percent higher than the Americans in the period when they were surging ahead of this country technologically. **T**he evidence is plain: like the managers at Penn Central who did so much to destroy the American rail system, the leaders in auto and steel proved themselves utterly inept, to the detriment not simply of the individual workers fired or laid off as a result, but of entire communities, cities, states and regions. And yet it remains an unassailable and incontrovertible fact for most Americans that the private sector is, of necessity, by its very nature, efficient. Adam Smith, it is wrongly thought (for Smith actually was against corporations and made his predictions on the basis of an entrepreneurial economy), showed for once and for all that railroad, auto and steel executives make the wisest choices, and that over a period of three decades, they will, with occasional errors, serve the common interest. Eventually, I am convinced, reality—which clearly shows that the problem, not the solution, is to be found in the boardroom—will subvert the hold of the American anti-ideology. And at that point it will occur to people that basic decisions about the very structure and future of the American economy—whether the steel valleys of Pennsylvania shall be economically and socially destroyed; whether entire neighborhoods in Detroit will be gutted—have to become public and involve worker, community and political representatives in the choices.

That new consciousness, so essential to the next America, will not emerge easily or automatically. What we call the New Deal —social security, union recognition, welfare and the like—did not come into being until late in Roosevelt's first term—i.e., six or seven years after the roof collapsed onto American capitalism. It took the greatest breakdown of the system in its entire history to get the government not to socialize the economy or anything like it, but merely to intervene through fiscal and monetary policy to provide sufficient demand so that corporations could make their inexorably wise decisions. Indeed, if the New Deal was politically radical, developing by means of fierce class struggles and political assaults on the "economic

Overleaf:
The public owns one fifth of the land in the United States. Genuine conservatives—like Theodore Roosevelt and Gifford Pinchot—fought for a national park system, created in 1916, to "conserve the natural and historic objects in such manner as will leave them unimpaired for the enjoyment of future generations." That dream has been real for more than half a century and is now under threat.

State park near Kitty Hawk, North Carolina, 1980

Brant, Jamaica Bay Wildlife Refuge, Gateway National Park, Queens, New York, 1981

royalists," it was actually moderate to conservative in its content and quite pious in its reverence for the Adam Smithian certitudes. The rich fought Roosevelt's attempt to save them from themselves, another example of how ideology can blind "practical" people to their own self-interest. And that fact suggests another ideological aspect of the present situation: that corporate leaders, who dominate the economy and disproportionately shape our politics, honestly believe that they are being victimized by big government. I had some personal contact with this attitude in 1980. It was a sign of the intensity of the economic crisis in that year that some important corporate types paid attention to what I was saying and even sought me out. In Memphis in the spring I delivered a lecture endowed by a prestigious accounting firm and had breakfast with some of the leading bankers of the city; in Pittsburgh I talked to, and then dined with, the top officials of the Mellon Bank at a seminar sponsored by the Carnegie-Mellon Business School; and in Colorado, at the Keystone Conference Center, I spent a week talking to public-affairs staff people from major corporations at a meeting organized by the Public Affairs Council. If these pillars of the corporate establishment were listening rather respectfully to what I had to say, it can be fairly assumed that they are profoundly nervous about the future. That could be a good sign. What I learned through those encounters, and particularly during the Colorado discussions, was what business people mean when they conjure up an America in which omnipotent government bureaucrats harass innocent executives. There are three agencies which they detest and regard as proof of the bureaucratic domination of their lives: the Occupational Safety and Health Administration, the Environmental Protection Ad-

Coal miner, West Virginia, 1977

Her father died of lung cancer after working in an asbestos factory. She used to wash his work clothes and two months after this photo was taken she died of lung cancer. The autopsy found traces of asbestos in her lungs.

Mrs. Van Zile, Paterson, New Jersey, 1974

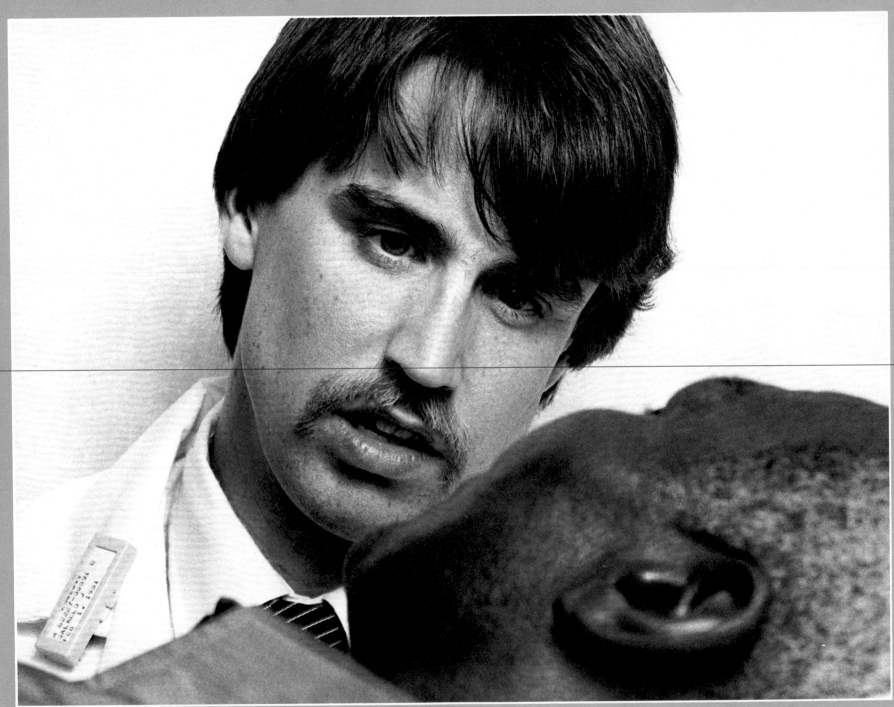

Doctor examining patient, Veterans' Hospital, Washington, D.C., 1981

ministration and the Equal Employment Opportunity Commission. **T**hose three institutions all have a common link. They all attempt to require the private sector to pay the actual costs of doing business rather than allow them to impose huge social costs—maimed bodies and lungs, death, pollution, racial and sexual discrimination—on the society as a whole. In each of those cases, the corporations had refused to "internalize" (to pay for) their "external diseconomies" (the destruction or injustice or inconvenience) they forced on their neighbors and customers. Part of their attitude is built into the system. If any one company decides to be more responsible about such evils, it will have to accept high costs because of its minimal decency. Then, all other things being equal, it will become less competitive than its antisocial rivals and will lose part of the market or even be driven into bankruptcy. Thus caring for the environment or workers' safety or sexual and racial equality is stupid within the logic of the system. That is why the government has to require all companies to meet norms. **T**here is no question that those agencies sometimes make bad bureaucratic decisions, and I discovered in 1980 that every business person has a small library of horror stories. Even discounting for self-interested exaggeration, there is some truth to the charges. For instance, the most enthusiastic defenders of occupational safety and health freely admit that OSHA made some overzealous, nitpicking errors in its early days. But what, then, is the alternative? To allow corporations to poison the land, the water, the sky, the work force, and to effectively enforce patterns of racial and sexual discrimination? **T**here is no bureaucrat in Washington—no bureaucracy in its entirety—which ever behaved as foolishly as the executives of the

The Veterans' Administration runs the largest hospital system in the United States and many public-health experts believe that its care is as good as that found in private-sector hospitals. The National Institutes of Health have been a critical source of medical innovation and research for years.

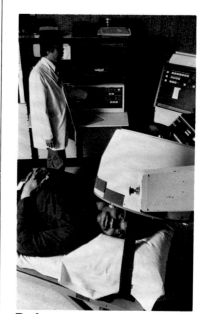

Brain scanner,
Veterans' Hospital,
Washington, D.C., 1981

American auto, steel and rail industries. Yet the latter, because of the hold of our anti-ideological ideology, still have a certain trust; the former do not. In part, of course, that is no accident but an artifact created by the executives from the auto, steel and rail industries and their brothers (and occasionally now, sisters) in other boardrooms. But in part it is also the result of a genuine confusion among the mass of people. In that context, I am not only amused and flattered and hopeful about corporation leaders talking to me, I am also afraid. Let me explain why. **I**n the thirties, the rich were, as I said earlier, unbelievably dense about their own interests. Indeed, if the capitalists had been allowed to run capitalism on their own during the Depression they probably would have destroyed it, something the workers were unable to accomplish. But this time around the executives are sadder and somewhat wiser. They are listening to socialist intellectuals like me from time to time. Even more to the point, they are recognizing the existence of a deep crisis, so that in 1980 the word *reindustrialization* became ubiquitous. On the one hand this term indicates that the rich have understood that the American crisis is structural, not cyclical, and that some rather far-reaching changes are going to be made. That, I suppose, is a gain if only because the truth is being stated. But, on the other hand, the new is therefore being proposed under the auspices of the old, and that is not good. **L**et me be specific. In a book on "pension-fund socialism" called *The Unseen Revolution*, Peter Drucker, a management ideologist, shrewdly recognized that corporate executives were more and more perceived, by the public as well as by the workers in their companies, as without real legitimacy. Therefore, Drucker said (and this is obviously my opinionated paraphrase of his much more diplomatic presentation), some semblance of

The government does not just spend money; it makes some of the most finely designed and executed bills in the world. As with the technology for lunar exploration and the space shuttle, Washington is capable of doing difficult jobs well.

Hand engraving a printing plate, U.S. Treasury Department, Washington, D.C., 1981

Trimming currency, U.S. Treasury Department, Washington, D.C., 1981

shared power must be allowed to the workers precisely in order to shore up the authority of the managers. That was the thrust of *Business Week*'s special issue on reindustrialization in the summer of 1980, of Felix Rohatyn's proposal for a new Reconstruction Finance Corporation and of many other blueprints for manipulated, controlled, top-down changes in the American system. They talked of a new "social contract," which almost always turns into billions of dollars of tax expenditures for the corporations—to give them sufficient cash flow to make the brilliant decisions which they are fated to make in our anti-ideology if not in real life—and calls on the workers and communities to trust that they will be the beneficiaries as those moneys trickle down to them. **S**o it is, for instance, that whenever there is talk of making the workers the owners of industry in order to enlist their enthusiasm and productivity, what is proposed is private, individualistic ownership. Employee Stock Ownership Plans (ESOP) are already favored in the federal law, not the least because Senator Russell Long is for them. They give each employee a share or two of stock, which confers on them the same social and economic decision-making power enjoyed by all small stockholders in huge enterprises: none. **I**ndeed in 1980 there was a strike by workers against a company which they "owned." The South Bend Lathe Corporation had been taken over by a trust when it was about to go bankrupt in the mid-seventies. In theory, the people who worked there then owned the enterprise. Typically, that ownership was exercised by the trust; the employees had no say over "their" property. **T**hat fraud was functional for about two years. The workers disbanded their local of the steelworkers union, convinced that they no longer needed to organize against a company they owned;

"Sesame Street" set, New York City, 1978

124

"Sesame Street" set, New York City, 1978

productivity went up by 25 percent. But then the reality—the total absence of effective ownership—became more and more apparent. The local union was reorganized and eventually had to strike the worker-"owned" company.

At the national level, in August 1980, the executive council of the AFL-CIO, in a dramatic reversal of a hallowed American labor tradition opposing any involvement in management decisions, came out in favor of getting union control over those billions of pension-fund dollars owned and invested in the name of, but almost never by, the workers. And during that same year, Douglas Fraser, the president of the auto workers, was elected to the board of Chrysler as part of the contract settlement with that ailing company. As a result of Fraser's presence, Chrysler became the first American corporation to have a management committee to study the problem of plant closings as it related to employees and their communities. So the notion of the democratic control of investment in the next America is not a utopian vision of a radical social critic. It has a political basis in the American trade-union movement. The unions? Of all my hopeful attitudes the one which is most controversial—in middle-class society at least—is my conviction that the unions have an enormously progressive role to play in this country. Even the "rediscovery" of the working class in the seventies took place by way of caricatures: Archie Bunker, the reactionary, racist, lovable oaf; or, among some on the Left, the countercaricature of the rank-and-filer as a militant Marxist who is kept from acting on his/her convictions only by conservative labor bureaucrats. But the actual functioning of the unions was *terra incognita* for most Americans. That became news only when there was violence or corruption. The largely fair and honest life of the biggest democratic movement in the nation might

Unemployed, State Unemployment Office, Dearborn, Michigan, 1981

Assembly line, Ford Motor Company, Dearborn, Michigan, 1981

as well have taken place on the far side of the moon.

Over the years, I have been one of the very few intellectuals in the United States who related to, and participated in, that unknown mass movement of working people. In the thirties and forties it would have been axiomatic that a middle-class Leftist would look to the working class for leadership, but that changed after World War II. Indeed, the radical, college-educated generation of the sixties was often as contemptuous of and hostile toward unions as they were toward corporation presidents. So my dogged commitment to labor made me old-fashioned in the eyes of many of those youthful rebels. But it also allowed me to grasp some of the enormous potential—and the problems and contradictions—to be found on that far side of the moon located in the plants and factories of the United States. Three recent events in that ongoing experience might help explain why I am both realistic and hopeful about the unions.

In 1977 I went out to the UAW educational center in Black Lake, Michigan, to talk to an educational conference of about three hundred local union leaders from Wisconsin and Minnesota. Ray Majerus—then a UAW regional director and later elected secretary-treasurer of the entire international union at the 1980 convention—had invited me as part of an imaginative experiment. I would not be introduced, he told me, as the author of *The Other America* or as an activist who worked with the UAW on many political projects. I would be presented as a socialist to see how these Middle American union members would respond to that fact. When I arrived, Ray told me that some of the people there had protested my being asked. For them—for the overwhelming majority of American workers—a socialist is either a Stalinist totalitarian or a middle-class dilettante who thinks he or she knows what is good for the workers better than they do.

Ray persisted, I was introduced as a socialist, and I spoke. At the end of the talk, there was a standing, enthusiastic ovation. More to my point, two men came up to me and told me that they had been among those who protested my being there. "What we can't understand now," one of them said, "is why we agreed with everything in your speech." **T**here are, I have long thought, people in America who are democratic socialists without knowing it, or are even under the misapprehension that they are antisocialists. Their ideas and their emotions are deeply anticorporate; the solutions they want are egalitarian and require the democratizing of investment decision. But American culture does not allow them to even know the proper name of their own ideology. I am not obsessed by labels, even though I do think that this country will never get even a thoroughgoing liberalism until socialism becomes an option in the mainstream. My point here is simply that if the eighties are as problematic as I think they will be, the scales may fall from millions of eyes, much as they did in the thirties, and working-class radicalism could once again become a creative force in the society. **T**hat will not happen as a simple, linear progression, a fact which was reinforced for me when I spoke at the UAW convention in 1980. I was introduced by Martin Gerber, a UAW vice-president, an avowed socialist and a friend. Martin is from a mold unfamiliar to most Americans: he is a working-class intellectual. He—and other trade-union friends of mine like Doug Fraser and Brendon Sexton of the auto workers, Bill Winipisinger from the machinists, Jerry Wurf of the state county and municipal employees—received a postgraduate ed-

**Assembly line,
Ford Motor Company,
Dearborn, Michigan, 1981**

Robotic welding machine, Ford Motor Company, Dearborn, Michigan, 1981

ucation in the course of fighting for workers' rights. They are better informed on many economic and political issues than almost any of the Ph.D.s I have known in those fields. Yet some of them did not graduate from high school. **A**t the 1980 UAW convention, though, there were those asking if men like Gerber and Fraser and Sexton were the last of a vanishing breed. The union has a strict rule that no one can be elected to office after his or her sixty-fifth birthday. Indeed at this convention two of the most important leaders—Irv Bluestone, one of the most thoughtful men in the American labor movement, and Emil Mazey, a legendary militant—were retiring. And when the UAW delegates meet in 1983 literally the entire Reuther generation will be forced out by the age rule. I knew the men and women who were slated to replace them and felt that the Reuther tradition would continue. But for how long? And would there be a new generation of working-class intellectuals, of people who acquired theoretical depth out of practical necessity? **O**ne theory said that the breed was indeed vanishing. In the thirties, this thesis goes, many of the most talented and imaginative young workers had to rise with their class rather than out of it for the simple reason that there were not enough openings up the ladder and, in any case, the Depression made a job—any job—a necessity. But in the postwar period, the argument continues, the number of "middle-class" jobs more than doubled and the portion of young people going to college quadrupled. Therefore, it is concluded, the Gerbers, Frasers and Sextons of the seventies and eighties will be found in college, not on the factory floor, and those who remain behind will have less capacity for leadership. **I** am not convinced. It is clear from my personal friendship with the union intellectuals I have

United Auto Workers Local meeting, Detroit, Michigan, 1981

United Auto Workers Local meeting, Detroit, Michigan, 1981

described that they are men of enormous natural ability. Yet their remarkable personal careers are also a social product. If they helped shape the progressive industrial unions which have been the most dynamic factor in the labor movement, those unions helped shape them. There are potential people of this sort in plants and offices today. Whether they realize that potential depends on events. Again, if I am right that the eighties will be a time of change and challenge, it will, like the thirties, create the conditions for a completely new generation of working-class intellectuals, many of them black, brown and female. **E**ven so, I was aware of the problems of the labor movement at that UAW convention in 1980. With a generational shift in process, and several hundred thousand workers on the street even as we were meeting, it would have been absurd to indulge in a kind of social romanticism. And the events surrounding my own speech brought that fact home to me quite forcefully. When I came to the rostrum there was a smattering of applause, but more than a few of the delegates seemed puzzled as to what I was doing there, particularly since Gerber had introduced me—and identified himself—as a socialist. I was frank about my politics, and I reminded the delegates that all three of the Reuther brothers had been socialists and that Victor, the last of the three, was a leading member of the socialist organization I chair.

United Auto Workers Local meeting, Detroit, Michigan, 1981

And then I launched into a sharp attack on the corporate priorities which allow boardrooms to close down plants and destroy communities in the name of a private "right" to balance the books. I advocated a broader public sector, a TVA-type energy corporation, worker and public seats on the boards of directors of all major corporations—in short, the democratization of corporate power. As the speech went on—it lasted about twenty minutes—I was interrupted by applause; when I ended, there was a warm, loud, standing ovation. After that, I left the hall to have a cup of coffee with Jimmy Herman, the leader of the West Coast longshoremen. **W**hen I returned, more than a little pleased with myself, I was greeted with the news that the convention had just spontaneously voted against a leadership proposal to remove the constitutional clause barring Communists and fascists from union office. The reason was a deep, visceral hatred of Communism. In other words, the delegates had proceeded from an ovation for the first American socialist to address such a meeting in years to an old-fashioned, emotional refusal of a civil liberties position put forward by their own leaders. My point is that the workers are complicated human beings with a radical, and a conservative, potential. **T**he last of these recent experiences with the labor movement underscores this complexity. In September 1980 I spoke to about forty construction workers, all black or Hispanic, in a shabby, but carefully tended, storefront in the South Bronx. They were members of the United Tremont Trades, a militant group that goes to "shape-ups" in order to get their members work in the South Bronx (where tearing down abandoned buildings is a perverse, but paying, business). I was invited by José Rivera and Edgar Cardona, two UTT leaders with whom I had worked earlier in the years in organizing a Left pressure at the Democratic convention. **I** made a talk about socialism. What struck me was how "American" the questions were afterward. One black wanted to know if socialism might not provoke violence and worried that the present, unjust and manifestly imperfect system might be preferable to any uncertain possibility I could conjure up. Another wondered if socialism would lower productivity and the desire to work.

Worker, United Tremont Trades, South Bronx, New York, 1981

José Rivera at Charlotte Street, South Bronx, New York, 1981

Here, just as with those unionists who protested my speaking at Black Lake, was powerful testimony to the influence of the capitalist ideology in the consciousness of people living in one of the most terrible ruins of the capitalist system. And yet these were militant workers who, at the end of an exhausting day, came to the storefront to plan more challenges to established authority. **O**bviously, then, my commitment to, and hopes for, the working people of this country is based on a realism which must endure more than a little ambiguity. I am not suggesting that the workers will inevitably and inexorably move to the left because of the economic crises of the eighties. But I am saying, with a personal knowledge of the contrary trends, that this is a very real possibility. **L**et me add yet another difficulty for this perspective. Even if my highest hopes for the labor movement were fulfilled, that would not guarantee the fulfillment of my hopes for the next America. The unions are the most important, organized source of power for such a transition; they are also only 20 percent of the labor force and more likely to decline slightly in the coming period than to make dramatic gains. Therefore I have thought and written for years that coalitions are the only way to progressive change: of women, one of the most important social movements of the seventies, and minorities and environmentalists and all of the other people whose dissatisfaction is positive. I will not try to make an exhaustive catalogue of the components of this new political alignment—I have done that elsewhere—and indeed I will focus on only one of its constituents: the college-educated, issue-oriented people who first appeared in the civil rights and antiwar movements of the sixties. They are, of course, a factor in some of the groups I have already mentioned—the feminist and the environmentalist cadres come from precisely this stratum—

**New housing,
South Bronx, New York, 1981**

and they are, like everything in this transitional time, ambiguous. My point here, as with the labor movement, is to evoke a source of social and political energy, not to analyze it or develop detailed strategies for it. There was a mass demonstration against President Carter's draft registration proposal in front of the Capitol in Washington in March 1980. After a cold, damp beginning on the Ellipse across from the White House that morning—where the red flags and stunning graphics of a slightly mad Maoist sect were the most cheerful note—we marched, between forty and fifty thousand strong, to the traditional rallying place on the steps right in front of the Senate and House. I was concerned that this new movement might become exclusively white, middle-class, self-righteously against a military service which was then imposed by means of cruel economic necessity, on blacks and Hispanics who are poor. I said that to the crowd. I also thought it important to make it clear that we were not a front movement for the Russian foreign office or, more to the point, for the imperialist invasion of Afghanistan by Soviet forces. I said that, too. And finally, I didn't want this effort to be seen as anti-American. So I said that we were in the best of American traditions—of Frances Wright and of Gene Debs and Margaret Sanger—and I concluded by quoting my friend Norman Thomas at one of the first Washington rallies against the war in Vietnam, in 1965. We are here, I argued, not to burn the American flag but to cleanse it. And that primarily young crowd which had materialized from out of the silent seventies and supposedly had little political sophistication roared its approval of those complex ideas for an antidraft movement. Again, there is no point in exaggerating. If the conventional judgment that the youth movement

**United Tremont Trades,
South Bronx, New York, 1981**

of the sixties went up in thin air during the seventies is false—and it is—that does not mean that college students and graduates are about to enlist, en masse, in the coalition I envision. That, not so incidentally, did not happen in the activist sixties, when the average student, at the very best, might have participated in one demonstration. Fewer than a hundred thousand youths put their stamp on a collegiate generation of more than seven million, but then every social movement is composed of a small vanguard and a much larger mass. What I am arguing is that this stratum is a potential source of energy for the next America I am suggesting here. That it is also capable of moralistic posturing, self-seeking hedonism and a dozen other cultural-political sins goes almost without saying. **T**ake the giant antinuclear rally in Washington in May 1979, shortly after the accident at Three Mile Island nuclear plant. Perhaps 100,000 people were mobilized after a mere six weeks of organizing, a feat which rivaled anything done in the sixties (when some demonstrations were bigger but had a much longer lead time). I spoke early on that day, down by the Ellipse and before the crowd moved up to the Capitol. There were "only" about 40,000 present at that point. I started by saying that the problems of opposition to nuclear energy were more complex than many imagined, pointing out that if all of that industry were shut down, over 100,000 workers would lose their jobs. Those people, I argued, would fight us unless we also favored a full-employment alternative which would put them to work creating a new solar technology. **W**hen I said that 100,000 would be jobless if there were a rapid transition to a non-nuclear world, a young man in the audience standing near some of my friends shouted out, "Tough!" This is the attitude of the college-educated activists which rightly drives some of

Director Freeman, member TVA Board, at public meeting, Clinton, Tennessee, 1981

When Barry Goldwater seemed to advocate selling the TVA to private enterprise in the 1964 campaign, Lyndon Johnson told a Memphis audience, "I can't sell it because I don't own it. You own it." The public has the right to attend the board of directors' meetings and to complain about overall policy, rates, or the effect of the water level behind the dams on fishing.

Citizen questioning TVA Board at public meeting, Clinton, Tennessee, 1981.

Trout fishing, Norris Dam, Tennessee Valley Authority, Norris, Tennessee, 1981

View from Norris Dam, Tennessee Valley Authority, Norris, Tennessee, 1981

Control room operator, Tennessee Valley Authority, Watts Bar nuclear plant, 1981

Street of brownstones, Bedford-Stuyvesant, Brooklyn, New York, 1980

Some urban revivals "gentrify" on behalf of the middle and upper-middle class, pushing the poor and minorities out of sight and mind; at least one revival, in Bedford-Stuyvesant, Brooklyn, New York, actually helped the poor and minorities. And all of these efforts show that unplanned and chaotic city change is not a fate but a choice—and that other choices, even socially responsible choices, are possible.

the best trade unionists into a fury. It is narrow, irresponsible, cruel, and it derives from a privileged social class position in society; it is the response of the secure, affluent young who have never been on an unemployment line. But then when I went on to say that there was a way in which those disemployed nuclear workers could get jobs in a rationally planned energy system, that same young man called out, "OK." Better late than never. **I**ndeed, there is a massive tendency in the politics of this stratum to link social radicalism and economic conservatism. In Jerry Brown's second inaugural, the young governor—and, at that point, Presidential candidate—came out for gay rights and a constitutionally mandated balanced budget. In the 1980 campaign, John Anderson, who had a major impact on campus in the fall of the year, similarly advocated progressive positions on the draft, foreign policy, women's rights, and stood by his essentially conservative past with regard to economic questions. If this trend turns out to be dominant among the educated activists, then there is no possibility of alliance with the unionists or the minorities—and little possibility that there will be any political coalition to save America from its present, painful bewilderment. But if these very same people look to the economics of their social radicalism, understanding that stagflation subverts the very best affirmative-action program for minorities and women, for instance, then new alignments are possible. **I** am saying two cheers, to borrow from E. M. Forster, not three. Two cheers for the accomplishments of the past, the imperfect but real gains of social security and civil rights. But only two cheers because every solution is ambiguous. A Tennessee Valley Authority is magnificent in producing cheap electric power, controlling floods and improving the economic climate of an entire region and it has a miserable record on the

Neighborhood workers painting block, Bedford-Stuyvesant, Brooklyn, New York, 1978

Restoration Plaza, Bedford-Stuyvesant, Brooklyn, New York, 1978

environment, not the least because over a period of two decades (from the early fifties to the mid-seventies) it adopted private corporate priorities as a guide to the policies of a public corporation. **A**nd yet I still say two cheers because I have been to Bedford-Stuyvesant and seen the present working just a little bit. The streets there are lined with elegant, well-kept brownstones which could easily serve as a backdrop for a Henry James novel about upper-middle-class life at the turn of the century. Only, they are found in the middle of New York's largest black ghetto. On the periphery of this Shangri-La—most dramatically in the Bushwick section to the north—the scenery is more typical of the times: an urban war zone of burned-out and abandoned buildings rotting in the aftermath of the power failure and riots of the summer of 1977. But in Bedford-Stuyvesant there was hardly any looting.

All this did not just happen. The white middle class moved out of Bed-Stuy in the period after World War II; the blacks who settled there when they came up from the South to work in the Brooklyn Navy Yard during the war stayed on, but the jobs disappeared. In 1967, a New York University study said that "Bedford-Stuyvesant is more depressed and impaired than Harlem—i.e., fewer unified families, more unemployment, lower incomes, less job history." And yet there were some positive data, too. About 22 percent of the brownstones were still owner-occupied; another 9.7 percent of the houses were owned by people who lived in close proximity to them.

Enter Robert Kennedy, then moving further to the left than any American politician before or since. It was almost inevitable that he would want to do something basic about black poverty, an issue that combined two of the central social concerns of the decade. And there were other, nonideological

**Restored houses,
Savannah, Georgia, 1979**

East Wing, National Gallery, Washington, D.C., 1980

Metro, Washington, D.C., 1981

reasons for wanting to do something about Bedford-Stuyvesant. It had become painfully clear that we could not have both guns and butter, because of the war in Vietnam; tapping private funds in an economic development project thus might deal with a serious new problem. **N**ot so incidentally, the whole undertaking might also provide Kennedy with a pro-business image for a Presidential campaign, something sorely needed by the man who had sent FBI agents to wake up steel-corporation executives during a crisis in his brother's administration. Indeed, there was a peculiar convergence of Left and Right in the notion of community development, and that, too, must have been politically attractive. To militant black-power advocates it meant local control of local resources and, in some of the more extreme images, a fantasy of socialism in one neighborhood. Those themes also spoke to the radicalizing white young in Students for a Democratic Society. At the same time, the scheme fit in with the new theories of black capitalism, and William Buckley endorsed the Kennedy initiative, noting that he had thought of it first.

The Kennedy name and power attracted support from the city's *haute bourgeoisie*: Thomas Watson of IBM; Douglas Dillon, the former Treasury secretary; George Moore of First National City Bank; and Benno Schmidt of J. H. Whitney and Company. Yet all that moneyed *noblesse oblige* did not guarantee the success of the project. What Kennedy did do before he was tragically gunned down in Los Angeles was to organize the community of Bedford-Stuyvesant itself. There were ferocious in-fights, and the first Restoration Corporation had to be reorganized before it was organized in the first place. But even that event was something of a blessing in disguise. It testified to the fact that people cared enough to battle over their own future.

Kennedy was murdered but the work went on. You walk down Fulton Street and there is a red tenement façade floating alongside a modern building. Next door, there is a converted milk-bottling plant, which had been abandoned for eight years before the planners took it over. Banners flap in the wind and you pass through an entryway which opens under the façade into a courtyard ringed by a new structure which contains shops and offices. The mood is not unlike that of a suburban shopping center, only more restrained and tasteful. That space flows into another plaza, with a skating rink. Beyond that, there is a low-rise housing development, also put up by the Restoration Corporation. In good weather, all these public spaces can be, and are, used for picnicking, concerts and the like. Across the street, a series of apartments encircles a garden. Solar equipment is being installed. In the neighborhood around the center, there are those marvelous blocks of intact brownstones.

The Restoration Corporation helped restore the brownstones, using local labor to do the job, for the most part (and working with the unions). It struggled to bring business into the area, including an IBM plant, which provided four hundred places for the community's workers. It supported small business and it ran social services. Most important of all, these various efforts engendered a community spirit which made Bedford-Stuyvesant relatively impervious to the rioting that took place during the summer of 1977.   **I**s this oasis in the Brooklyn slums really Shangri-La? Not at all. There are still many, many problems in Bed-Stuy. By dint of enormous effort, the Restoration Corporation managed to find a new plant site for IBM and to keep the factory from moving. But that is the only major company that has located in the area.

Renaissance Center, Detroit, Michigan, 1981

And Franklin Thomas, the man who directed the corporation during its first decade, freely admits that, for all the gains, another major downturn in the American economy could well reverse some of the happy trends he and his associates helped set in motion. It is a critical truth of these times that there is no place to hide from the complexities and agonies of the society. Bedford-Stuyvesant is no exception to that rule.

So let me state my point *sotto voce*. All that Bedford-Stuyvesant shows is that a mobilization of poor people within the context of a serious plan and with major political support can work. That is all—and that is everything. For it means that the decisions ahead in the eighties are choices, not inevitabilities. My two cheers, then, are justified. There is a vision of the economic basis of the next America. Where the New Deal trusted in the Adam Smithian wisdom of the boardroom and only intervened in order to create the conditions in which, say, the rail, auto and steel industries would make their efficient choices, experience has taught us that democratizing that investment process is not simply good and participatory, but essential if we are to make the structural changes the times require. And there is the possibility that significant— potentially, majority—social forces will understand that such a transformation is in their own interest as well as that of the nation as a whole. If enough people realize that this possibility exists, then it might just become real. Therefore, two cheers. And the alternative to those two cheers? Not, I insist, Ronald Reagan's utterly sincere, utterly irrelevant vision of a new city on the hill, but Disney World. That is the next America which Reagan and his friends have placed on the agenda: a reactionary and very modern future in the fantastic costume of a dead past. In our 1984, perhaps Cinderella's Castle will look down on us rather than a portrait of Big Brother. Our national model will be a small town fraudulently concocted by a huge corporation; a celebration of free enterprise within the confines of a perfect monopoly; a homely, reverential, authoritarian and corporate-dominated place; a society managed by a sophisticated business elite but pretending to be a laissez-faire utopia. George Orwell's Mickey Mouse. **B**ut because that frightening possibility exists, there is reason to hope. These times of in-between are profoundly unsettling, the result of long-range trends which have been burrowing in our history for centuries, which undermine some of our basic social and cultural and religious institutions and which now converge with the most severe structural economic problems since the Great Depression. If, as is almost always the case—including in 1929—the first impact of these dislocations is to drive people to the right, to me-firstism and nostalgia, its more lasting effect could well be to awaken people to new possibilities born of new necessities.

The historical basis of those traditional virtues which are now being so desperately, despairingly and militantly proclaimed by the Right was a revolutionary process which sharply increased the autonomy of vast numbers of people. The rise of capitalist democracy was anything but a simple linear process. Nevertheless, through bitter struggles, not simply the capitalists, but a new middle class and then a new working class conquered a space for themselves. They did not wish those values into existence; they fought for them against the established power. **T**he conservative agenda for the 1980s is unwittingly, implicitly, radical, which is to say that conservatives cannot carry it out. To propose work for all in an economy which now regards 7 percent unemployment as "good times" is to demand national economic planning and social investment. If such work is to be human and enriching—which is how work in the past is remembered with utter inaccuracy—in a society where robots and routine service jobs are on the increase, that only means an exponential increase in the challenge. And the same holds for the search for community in a country which has reduced so many neighborhoods to rubble, and for stable families in a time of mindless hedonism. I do not pretend for a minute that I rejoice in the triumph of so many Rightists in 1980, that I advocate decline in order to stimulate rise. That is almost as dangerous and delirious a thought as the German Communist slogan of 1932–33, "After Hitler Comes Us," the notion that nazism would simplify the choices. Indeed, I spent several years trying to convince the democratic Left that traditional liberalism was finished, that it was necessary to go as far beyond Franklin Roosevelt as Roosevelt had gone beyond Herbert Hoover. I failed. Alas, it was conservatives who were the irreverent debunkers of ossified tradition in the early eighties.

But if Reagan and his friends were right about the need for radical new departures, they were cruel and wrong—and wrong because they were cruel—about what those departures should be. In his 1981 program, the President claimed that he would defend the rights of the "very needy"; meanwhile, he made a man who had written a book proving that there are no poor people in America his chief domestic advisor. And he attacked food stamps and Medicaid in order to make room for the tens of billions in subsidies to the corporate rich who were supposed to invest their welfare payments in employment-creating enterprises. That these were the same corporate rich who, in the last three years of the seventies, wasted $100 billion in acquiring and reacquiring existing assets without generating a single new job is but one of the many reasons why I am convinced this approach will not work. **A**nd strangely enough it is the impossible, mean radicalism of the Reagan administration which gives me some hope for the Left. New departures are indeed imperative, but not corporate Cinderella castles. The fantasy visions of a renascent conservatism respond to real needs which only the democratic Left can answer. And that is the ironic reason why I believe that the declines described in this book might—only, but emphatically, *might*—be the prelude to a new rise.